Ask a Footballer

JAMES MILNER

Ask a Footballer

My Guide to Kicking a Ball About

Written with Oliver Kay

Quercus

First published in Great Britain in 2019 by Quercus.

Quercus Editions Ltd
Carmelite House
50 Victoria Embankment
London EC4Y 0DZ

An Hachette UK company

A CIP catalogue record for this book is available
from the British Library

HB ISBN 978 1 52940 494 4
TPB ISBN 978 1 52940 495 1
Ebook ISBN 978 1 52940 493 7

10 9 8 7 6 5 4 3 2 1

Typeset by CC Book Production
Printed and bound in Great Britain by Clays Ltd, Elcograf S.p.A.

MIX
Paper from
responsible sources
FSC® C104740
FSC www.fsc.org

Papers used by Quercus are from well-managed forests and other responsible sources.

Contents

Introduction

I believe it's standard for a book of this type to begin with a shocking revelation, so here goes.

My name is James Milner and I'm not a Ribena-holic.

I don't really drink much tea either. I might have a few cups over the course of a week, but I actually prefer coffee.

And it gets worse. I can't iron.

Yes, I've been living a lie. Someone made a Twitter parody of me – making me out to be even more boring than I am – and I've enjoyed playing along with it. When we beat Roma to reach the Champions League final in 2018, the interviewer asked me on the pitch afterwards whether I might celebrate with an Italian red wine. Because I don't drink alcohol, I joked that I might stretch to a Ribena. That was the first thought that came into my head. And for some reason, it became a 'thing'. One day, a huge crate of Ribena arrived at the training ground for me. Any time I look at my mentions on Twitter, I've got people asking me about Ribena (and tea and ironing). Before the Champions League final, someone mocked up an image of me dreaming about myself flying over the stadium on a giant Ribena bottle with the European Cup in my hands. The caption read, 'Ribena for my men. We ride at dawn.'

When I stop to think about it, being a professional footballer in the modern era can be pretty weird at times. Weird that someone would go to the trouble of setting up that @BoringMilner account in my 'honour' and keeping it going for years. Weird that more than half a million people are so amused by jokes about me doing household chores and drinking tea (and I have to admit I find some of them funny myself). Weird that a throwaway remark in a post-match interview ends up with me being sent a load of Ribena. Definitely more than a bit weird that when I went onto social media to invite fans of all clubs to ask questions for me to answer in this book, so many of them were about Ribena, tea and ironing.

So, to @Collypool, @butterinthecup, @nighters84 and countless others, I'm afraid I will only be answering one question about Ribena. Yes @KrisMillsKJK and others, I can make a decent cup of tea (Yorkshire, obviously – and the milk definitely goes in second), but it's not something I can give you a great deal of insight about. To @CrispyCollins88, @MrKindle_85 and the many others who asked me about ironing, I'm ashamed to say I haven't a clue. I don't even know how to turn it on.

What I can shed some light on, I hope, is what it's like being a professional footballer, how it felt to break into the first team at Leeds back in 2002, six months after taking my GCSEs. And I can give some insight into my different experiences with Newcastle, Aston Villa, Manchester City and now Liverpool (not forgetting a six-match loan spell at Swindon) as well as my highs and a few too many lows playing for England. There are still plenty of older lads knocking around – hi Jags – but there isn't another current one who has been playing Premier League football as long as I have. As the publishers of this book have managed to persuade me, that gives me a pretty rare insight into how the game has changed over the past 17 years.

And it really has. I'm not saying it was the dark ages when I started, but there were still a lot of very old-school attitudes at that time. Even after making my Premier League debut for Leeds, as a 16-year-old YTS lad, I still had to do all the odd jobs around the training ground – cleaning the first-team players' boots, picking their dirty slips off the dressing room floor, cleaning out the showers. That would be unthinkable now. There were a few analysts and fitness coaches around at the biggest clubs in those days, but you didn't have your performance, fitness and diet micro-managed like you do now. Dressing rooms were a very different place back then – louder and a lot wilder in terms of the banter that used to fly around. Mobile phones were common enough, but if you whipped one out in the dressing room or on the bus, you would be in trouble. You walk into any football club dressing room these days and almost all the players are on their phone or wearing headphones. It's much, much quieter.

In some ways, it's more relaxed. In other ways, the pressure now seems constant. Football these days can feel like it's 24/7. It has become more complicated. There's so much more swirling around than what happens in the 90 minutes. The media spotlight grew and grew in the first ten years of my career. Since then, it has really intensified with social media. It's very easy for players to believe they're the best thing since sliced bread when they win – and to feel useless or inadequate when they lose a match or when they're suffering from a long-term injury.

In this book, I'll try to explain how a footballer's working week unfolds – what we eat and how we prepare for matches technically, tactically, mentally and physically – and talk you through the ups and downs of a match day. I'll talk about how we try to stop ourselves going stir-crazy when we're away for three weeks on a pre-season tour. I'll answer questions about penalty-taking techniques, half-time team-talks and the differences between playing against Lionel Messi, Wilfried Zaha and Jimmy Bullard.

I'll also answer your questions about playing for different managers, ranging from Terry Venables, Peter Reid and Sir

Bobby Robson to Martin O'Neill, Fabio Capello and Jürgen Klopp. I'll tell you what it's like sharing a training ground and a dressing room with team-mates ranging from Lee Bowyer to Mario Balotelli to Mo Salah. I'll talk you through the first years of a glorious era at Manchester City and try to persuade @dave_bones that celebrating a goal against them didn't make me a 'snake'. I'll give you some insight into the behind-the-scenes work that went into Liverpool's Champions League success – and the celebrations that followed – and, at @jerry3089's request, I'll try to contemplate what my life would be like if I hadn't met Divock Origi. I'll answer one of the many Leeds fans who pointedly asked where I'm going to go if or when the time comes for me to leave Liverpool. There'll even be a few questions from the man who lifted the biggest trophy in club football on 1 June 2019: Mr @JHenderson.

This isn't an autobiography. The whole point of *Ask A Footballer* is that people can ask me what they like and I can use my own experiences to give a sense of what a footballer's day-to-day existence is like. It's mostly your questions, but we've come up with various others that enable me to explain different things that I wasn't directly asked about.

Of course you might end up thinking I'm even more boring than @BoringMilner, but maybe being boring has helped me keep going in the Premier League for 17 years (and counting). And maybe trying to stay the same over all that time – still the same lad from Leeds, still teetotal, still with the same girl and still with pretty much the same haircut – has made it easier for me to reflect on the changes I've seen in the game. It is still the same game, but it does feel very, very different from when I first started kicking a ball around Horsforth.

James Milner, Cheshire, October 2019

Early Days

How did you start playing footy? @Rampagingorange

I started playing at my school, Westbrook Lane Primary. It was absolute mayhem in the playground, with about ten different games going on at once and balls flying everywhere, but I must have been quite decent at that early age because we would often have games where it was me taking on the rest of my class. I then joined a local team, Westbrook Juniors, but becoming a professional footballer was the furthest thing from my mind. I was just playing because I enjoyed it.

My first ever game was a disaster. I was about eight years old, playing for Westbrook Juniors, and we lost 16–2. How can you lose 16–2? Well, it was the first game any of us had ever played. We had all kicked a ball around, but we had never even had a training session. We went with our mums and dads and we all met up in a pub car park somewhere. One of the parents said, 'Right, what position do you all play?' None of us had a clue. 'Who wants to be a striker?' That sounded great. Everyone put their hand up. 'Oh, right.'

We turned up at this place in Colton, on the other side of Leeds, and walked out onto this pitch that looked bigger than Wembley. Honestly, it must have been a full-size pitch with full-size goals, which is absolute madness when you're talking about under-nines. And we got absolutely spanked. I know I scored one of our goals and set up the other, but I don't remember anything else about it except feeling slightly bewildered. I'm pretty sure we only won two games all season. It wasn't a great start to my career.

When you were a kid, whose goal on the '101 Great Goals' VHS tape did you try to replicate the most down park whilst doing the BBC commentary? @bully185

Actually, my favourite video was *Leeds United: 180 Goals*, which was exactly what it said on the box – 180 Leeds United goals from the late 1960s all the way to 1990, so there was Billy Bremner, Alan Clarke, Mick Jones, Peter Lorimer and all those guys. I used to watch that all the time. My favourite goals were the two worldies that Eddie Gray scored against Burnley – one an outrageous chip from long distance and the other the maziest dribble you've ever seen. Eddie had been retired a long time by then and I ended up being lucky enough to play under him at Leeds. I don't think I ever told him I tried to recreate his goals.

I was totally into Leeds. My mum and dad took me to Elland Road from a very young age – so young that I can't remember what my first match was. I was only six when Leeds won the league in 1992. My memory of that is my dad going mad and whirling me around the living room, telling me to remember it because it might never happen again in my lifetime. I didn't have a clue what he meant at the time, but I understand now (although hopefully it will happen again one day).

We got season tickets a couple of years after that. They were great tickets, bang on the halfway line, halfway up the East Stand. I loved everything about it – the noise, the atmosphere and obviously what happened on the pitch too. One game that really sticks out in my mind was against Derby. We were 3–0 down early on and ended up winning 4–3, with Jimmy Floyd Hasselbaink equalising and then Lee Bowyer scoring the winner in the last minute. I didn't appreciate back then that there was such a thing as a Leeds–Derby rivalry – yes, it goes back a lot further than Marcelo Bielsa – but the place was bouncing that day. It was a brilliant game and an incredible atmosphere.

We went down to Wembley to watch Leeds in the Coca-Cola Cup final, which they lost against Aston Villa. We also watched Guiseley at Wembley in the FA Trophy final. We used to go to watch Guiseley quite a lot and we enjoyed it. But really it was all about Leeds for me.

Whose name did you have on the back of your shirt when you were growing up?

The first one, you probably wouldn't guess. It was Tony Dorigo. I told Andy Robertson that recently – and Robbo hadn't heard of him. Mind you, Robbo won't have heard of anyone unless they played for Celtic. But yes, Tony Dorigo. I'm starting to wonder whether I had some deep-rooted desire to be a makeshift left-back, but on reflection I think it was just because he was fast and he was a good player. I had Tony Yeboah after that. He was a real hero of mine. He scored a few worldies – the volley against Liverpool at Elland Road, that thunderbolt away to Wimbledon. I had a Lee Bowyer shirt at one point too. Alan Smith was one of my favourites, a local lad who had done what all of us in the academy wanted to do. I really liked Jimmy Floyd Hasselbaink, but I never had his shirt. You had to pay by the letter in those days, so maybe that's why my dad, a proper Yorkshire fella, steered me away from it.

Who was your football role model when you were younger? Whose playing style did you try to emulate that most aligned with your abilities or growth? @TuelLogan

I wouldn't say I had any one particular role model, or a player that I tried to emulate. There were different players I liked and I probably tried to take bits from all of them. I've mentioned Yeboah, Hasselbaink, Bowyer and Smith, but away from Leeds, I was a massive fan of Alan Shearer, particularly after Euro 96, and Gazza. I used to love getting up on Saturday mornings to watch Gazza playing for Lazio on *Gazzetta Football Italia*. Channel 4 was great on Saturday mornings: kabaddi, then *Transworld Sport*, then *Gazzetta*. They don't make Saturday morning TV like that any more.

How did you get signed by Leeds? Were other clubs interested?

The first club that showed an interest was Everton. I might even have ended up signing for them if my trial hadn't been called off because of snow.

I had carried on playing for Westbrook Juniors and I ended up moving up to the under-12s because they didn't have an under-10 or under-11 team. I was a lot smaller than the other kids, but I was very quick, believe it or not, and I didn't feel out of place. I scored a lot of goals and I must have been doing okay because when it came to the end of that season, there were parents from some of the other teams complaining that I shouldn't be allowed to play against them because I was 'too young'. Looking back, I'm not convinced that was the real reason they wanted me to drop down to my own age group.

I then got into the district team, which was Airedale and Wharfedale – 'Aire and Wharfe' to us. I played a district match in Crosby and I was told afterwards that an Everton scout had been watching and wanted me to go on trial.

That was the first time I had even thought about the possibility of being a footballer, but then the trial game got called off because of snow. We kept waiting for another phone call, but it never came, so I thought my chance might have come and gone.

Then, towards the end of that season, I was invited for a trial at Leeds. I had been doing well for the district team. I went along, was given the Leeds kit to play in and I played a trial game. That felt amazing. I was just starting to get into my stride when I was taken off. I thought, 'What have I done wrong?' My dad reckons they just wanted to give the opposition full-back a break.

I was invited to go back again, so I went in some casual gear, thinking I would be given the kit to play in again, and they told me, 'No, you were supposed to bring your own gear.' So for my first proper training session at Leeds, I had to wear some random-ass gear. Thinking about that, it's the kind of thing I would hammer a team-mate for these days at Liverpool. Turning up for training in the wrong gear would get you a massive fine. Luckily, at Leeds, I got away with nothing worse than a few strange looks.

I ended up signing schoolboy forms for Leeds. Not only that, but when I was 12, they told me I would get a four-year contract that would start on my 16th birthday. We were playing against all the other under-12 teams from all over the north of the country – Liverpool, Manchester United and so on – and it all suddenly felt very serious. I had played a lot of cricket before that and I was doing a lot of cross-country running, but it reached the stage where I became totally focused on trying to make it at Leeds.

What are some of the things your parents did to help you become so successful as a footballer? @el_guapo_blanco

My parents have been brilliant every step of the way. I know a lot of players didn't have this luxury, growing up in different parts of the world or even in the UK, but my parents always made sure I had boots and they used to drive me all over the place, which is something you don't even begin to appreciate at the time. When I was in the academy at Leeds, my dad would rush home from work in the evenings and then drive me to training at Thorp Arch, half an hour away, watch me train and then drive me home again afterwards. My mum always used to come and watch me play in school matches. I can remember one game, playing in driving hail, and seeing mum standing on the hill, getting pelted with hailstones as she watched me. Again, it's one of those things that you take for granted at the time, but appreciate more when you get older.

I spent a lot of time in the car with my dad and we would talk about the game, how I was doing and so on. He gave me positive feedback when I played well, but he also knew how to gee me up. One of my coaches, Colin Morris, said that if I didn't end up playing for England, he would eat his hat. It felt mad to hear a coach say something like that about me, but my dad always wanted me to keep my feet on the ground. He kept telling me I needed to carry on improving. He said that anything I could do with my right foot, I needed to be able to do with my left foot too. I spent so much time working on my left foot. I'll always be primarily right-footed, but I'm comfortable on my left now, which has made me a much better player and able to operate in several positions. A lot of that is down to my dad. It might just sound like basic advice, but I always felt that gave me an edge.

If people talk about good standards, I would say that was drummed into me by my dad. He would always insist I did my homework, cleaned my boots, all that kind of thing, and he knew how to motivate me. Sometimes he would say I wasn't dedicated enough. I had some really talented team-mates in the academy at Leeds. One of them, a lad called Ian Douglas, had amazing technique. He was small, but he was an Adam Lallana type and he could do kick-ups all day, that sort of thing. My dad used Ian as an example to motivate me. If I was watching TV, he would say, 'Do you think Ian Douglas is watching TV? No, he'll be out practising.' So I would go outside in a rage, booting the ball against the garage, and all that time spent practising made me an even better player. My dad wasn't doing it nastily or anything like that. He just knew how to give me a gee-up.

Who was the best player you played with or against at youth level?

Everton had a really good team. Their star player was a stocky centre-forward who was incredibly talented and was also one of the most physical players I had ever seen. We must have been playing under-12s when he was involved in a nasty collision with our centre-half, who got a horrific deep gash on his leg. For us, aged 11 or 12, it was sickening. It wasn't his fault, but we always remembered that kid at Everton and, because he was so good, we found it weird that, when we played against them the next year and the year after that, he was nowhere to be seen. It turned out he was already playing for the under-16s. Yes, you've guessed. Wayne Rooney.

The other one was Luke Moore, who went on to play for Aston Villa and West Brom. When I got called up for the England under-15 and under-16 squads, Luke was the star of that team. He was really talented and he was prolific at youth level. He already had a boot deal with Nike at 15, which to me was just amazing. Also in that team was Tom Huddlestone, who went on to play for the England senior team. He was one of the youngest in the team, but he was already massive and his passing was so good, it was just a joke. He could receive a bouncing ball and, first time, with either foot, hit a perfect 30-yard daisy-cutter out to the wide man. The captain was Steven Taylor, who was later a team-mate of mine at Newcastle. There was Tom Heaton, Jamie O'Hara, Grant Leadbitter and Dean Bowditch as well as Aaron Lennon, who was in the year below me at Leeds. I wasn't a regular starter in that team. When we played the Victory Shield, I came on for the last 15 minutes against Northern Ireland at Rushden & Diamonds' ground. I didn't play at all in the second game against Wales. The first time I started was against Scotland at Inverness. That was the first time I had ever encountered a hostile crowd away from home. They were booing the national anthem – at under-16 level! I'm guessing it was a seven-year-old Andy Robertson in the crowd who started it.

What were you like at school? Were you the teacher's pet or were you totally distracted by football?

I wouldn't say I was distracted by football. I wasn't allowed to be. My parents always said I wasn't allowed to play football unless I'd done my homework. I was training with Leeds at Thorp Arch two or three times a week, but I still had to find the time to do my homework.

I did pretty well in my GCSEs. I got something like one C, one B, six or seven As and an A*. The A* was in PE, which probably isn't that surprising. I enjoyed IT. I was okay at German – good enough to get an A. I remember bits of it, but I don't think I would try using it when chatting with the manager. Not unless I had to ask the way to the Bahnhof or the Kino, anyway. My worst subject was English. There was far too much essay-writing for my liking. I would always try to put it off until the last minute. I'm not sure I can blame that on being distracted by football. It's just human nature when you're a teenage boy.

What was your YTS apprenticeship at Leeds like?

I started at Leeds that summer, after my GCSEs. All the YTS lads lived at the training ground during the week. Those of us who lived locally came home at weekends. We had to do all the odd jobs around the training ground – cleaning everyone's boots, pumping up the balls, cleaning the showers, sweeping the dressing room and so on, all the things that young players these days aren't allowed to do because it's considered demeaning.

We had to grow up very quickly. But that YTS year was a bit different for me because, having started out training with the rest of my age group in the under-17s, I was then sent away to Scotland for pre-season with the under-19s. Then I was sent home after one game. One of the coaches said to me, 'It's just because you're going to be playing a lot of football this year.' That didn't seem to make sense. I thought I must have done something wrong.

To cut a long story short, I started training with the reserves and then Terry Venables had me training with the first team. I was training alongside Lee Bowyer, Harry Kewell, Alan Smith, all these great players I had idolised, and I was thinking, 'I cannot *believe* I'm in a passing circle with these guys.' The size of that jump, going from youth team to the ressies to the first team so quickly, was just ridiculous. The training was so much faster and more intense. I was fit, but I was blowing after five minutes. It was a huge step up, as a 16-year-old lad who had only just started his YTS, but I managed to get used to it.

Around the same time, Wayne Rooney broke into the Everton team and scored an unbelievable last-minute winner against Arsenal, five days short of his 17th birthday. Two weeks later Everton came to Elland Road and Wazza came off the bench to score a brilliant goal in front of the away supporters. I just remember thinking, 'Wow. He's doing it. Fair play to him. I just wish that was me.' I had just started training with Leeds' first team and I had actually been in the squad for that game – not the official squad but we had five subs and I was the 17th man in the squad in case anyone picked up an injury. One of the coaches turned to me at the end of the game and said, 'You're desperate to do what he's doing, aren't you? You're not far off, you know.'

The weekend after that, I was in the squad for a Premier League game at West Ham. It was the first time I'd been away with the first team and this time I was going to be on the bench. I was nervous as hell. We had started the season badly and were towards the bottom of the table, so I thought the only possible way I would get on was if we were winning comfortably or if we were losing so heavily that we had nothing to lose. We rushed into a 4–1 lead by half-time and I thought, 'I've actually got a chance of getting on here.' Then they pulled it back to 4–2 ('Probably not getting on') and then 4–3 ('Definitely not getting on') and, although the match was unbelievably frantic and tense, I probably started to relax a little bit on the bench, thinking I wasn't going to be needed.

And then, with us hanging on at 4–3 up with six minutes left, Terry Venables told me I was coming on for Jason Wilcox, which, looking back, was the sign of an incredibly brave manager. I stripped off and came on for my Premier League debut at Upton Park. I'm certain that none of West Ham's players – the likes of David James, Michael Carrick, Joe Cole, Jermain Defoe and Paolo Di Canio – had the slightest clue who I was. I'm not even sure some of my team-mates knew who I was. My dad, who was in the away end, said that even the Leeds fans were saying, 'Who the hell is this kid? He looks like he should be at school' – which a few months earlier I had been.

I had only just come on when Lee Bowyer passed it to me, to give me a nice early touch of the ball and settle me in. I tried to knock it back to him first time and – oh, jeez – it went straight to Di Canio 35 yards from goal. Di Canio pounced on it, dribbled forward and hit a shot that whistled just over the crossbar. I breathed a sigh of relief and the rest of the game passed without incident as we held on for a much-needed win. In the showers afterwards, Lee Bowyer said to me, 'F***ing hell, geez. Did you have a bet on 4–4 or what?' But the players were great with me afterwards. So was Terry Venables. He didn't have the best time of it at Leeds, but to throw on such a young player in those circumstances takes some balls. Eddie Gray was great with me too. I still had to pick everyone else's dirty slips and socks off the dressing room floor, though. Welcome to the big time, eh?

How did it feel to go from being an unknown 16-year-old to being all over the back pages when you became the youngest goalscorer of the Premier League era with that goal at Sunderland? Paul Handy

It felt mad. It still feels mad now, looking back at it. Over the next four or five weeks, I came on a few more times, but Terry Venables, Eddie Gray and the senior players were very good at helping me stay on an even keel. I had barely been mentioned in the media, which suited me down to the ground. It was the complete opposite of what Wazza was getting at Everton. I didn't envy him that.

On Christmas Day I travelled up to Sunderland with the first-team squad for the Boxing Day game. I was still a week away from turning 17, but I had played a few games and I didn't feel as nervous as I had at West Ham. This time my chance came early when I went on for Alan Smith in the first half, just after Sunderland had taken the lead. I had more time to get myself into the game, playing on the right of midfield as we pushed for an equaliser. And I just remember making a run across the near post as Jason Wilcox whipped a ball in low. I slid in and scored and went running to celebrate in front of the Leeds fans. I don't know how to describe my emotions at that point. It was a ridiculous feeling. Ridiculous.

Afterwards I was told that I had broken Wazza's record by five days to become the youngest Premier League goalscorer – 16 years and 356 days. It's hard to get your head round something like that. Thinking about it now, it's just weird. I saw a clip of that goal not long ago and my wife Amy said I looked like I was 12. I would have said more like 11, given how massive and baggy the shirt looked on me.

It got even better. Two days later I scored again, this time at home to Chelsea. People always talk about my goal at Sunderland, but the Chelsea one meant more to me because it was at Elland Road, in a big game, in front of our supporters. And also because it was a really nice goal. I turned away from Marcel Desailly and curled it past the keeper from just outside the box. My dad says everyone was going mad in the stands. Every fan loves to see their team score, but they love it even more when it's one of their own.

I had people asking for my autograph at the players' entrance afterwards. And then my mum and dad drove around to pick me up and take me home. We came home and watched it again on *Match of the Day* and at that point it was just, like, 'Ping, ping, ping, ping' on my phone as the messages came in. I was still 16, straight out of school, still earning £70 a week on YTS, and I was suddenly playing – and scoring – in the Premier League. Looking back now, that just seems ridiculous.

The phone didn't stop ringing. My parents' number was in the phone book, so anyone could track us down. There were journalists ringing up and knocking on the door, hoping for an interview, which I was never going to give, and there were agents clamouring to try to represent me. A few turned up at the cricket club over the road, asking whether James Milner lived around here. 'James Milner? No, never heard of him.' If they'd really been switched on, they might have noticed there were some pictures on the wall of me in the cricket team.

A few days after that, on my 17th birthday, we had an FA Cup game at Scunthorpe. The Leeds fans behind the goal

were singing 'Happy Birthday', which was quite surreal. In
the dressing room afterwards I was putting my trackie bot-
toms on and suddenly . . . 'Hang on, what's gone on here?'
My tracksuit and my trainers had all been cut up by the
senior players. As strange as it will sound, it made me feel
more accepted by them. But it was massively embarrassing.
The kitman wouldn't give me any other gear, because he
was in on it too, and the timing couldn't have been worse
because there was a bit of a buzz about me after the goals
I had scored that week. I had to go backwards and forwards
from the dressing room to the bus about five times because,
as a YTS lad, I was helping the kitman with the slips and
the kit. I walked out in the corridor and all the Scunthorpe
ball boys were staring at me, as if to say, 'Look at the state
of him.' When I walked out, there was a crowd outside next
to the bus. I'd been in the headlines that week, but people
hadn't really seen me before, so they were looking at me
as if to say, 'Is that *tramp* the kid who has just scored two
goals in the Premier League? What's going on?'

It would have been a fair question.

Training Ground:
Nutrition and Fitness

What was it like to be part of the transformation when football went from players eating Mars bars and smoking at half-time to PhD nutritionists and personal fitness regimes so good that even the back-up goalkeeper is now able to run 10 km for 90 minutes? @Antonstotle

Smoking at half-time? I'm not *quite* that old – although I've heard that Tugay used to like a half-time fag at Blackburn. And what a player he was. If I think back to 2002, when I started as a scholar at Leeds, things were a lot more advanced than they had been ten years earlier, when there were still some players having steak and chips for pre-match meals. By the time I started, there was a lot more emphasis on protein, steamed vegetables and so on, but there have still been a lot of changes over the past 17 years. Even if I consider how much it has improved over the course of my time at Liverpool, since the club brought in Mona Nemmer from Bayern Munich as our nutritionist, it's a big, big difference.

At Leeds there was a canteen at the training ground, which was probably pretty good by the standards of that time – lots of pasta, chicken, fruit and vegetables. But we would also have iced fingers for an afternoon snack every day and think nothing of it. And because, as YTS lads at Leeds, we lived at the training ground – yes, literally lived there – we would always head over for toast and cereal late at night. Or the lads would go to the garage down the road for a bag of sweets or crisps, which they would then go and eat in their rooms. I'm sure that kind of thing still happens at times, but nothing like as regularly as it did back then.

We have always seemed to go through different phases and fads with different nutritionists. At one of my previous clubs, we had one guy who came in and gave us all these supplements. It was the first time I'd experienced that. I found it way over the top. He would give us two different shakes – one was your fruit intake and one was your veg. The first was horrific and the second was even worse, the nastiest thing I've ever tasted. I could only manage it for three days. I remember struggling to force it down, standing over the sink before I went to bed. It was like one of those bushtucker trials. I feel sick even thinking about it.

The same nutritionist said we should only eat protein and no carbs. One player would rock up for training every morning and have a big steak for breakfast. It worked for him – he felt great on it – but I didn't feel so good and I went back to having carbs.

I'm not great with eating. A lot of the time, I eat because I have to, not for pleasure. What I've got much better at is forcing food down after a game because I know how important that is nutrition-wise. You end up finding out what's good for you. I've become more aware of that as my career has gone on.

The first year I was at Liverpool, the food after the game wasn't great and quite a few of the lads barely touched it. That was far from ideal because your post-match refuelling is very important. We had a chat about it and the manager and the staff agreed that it was better to eat something – almost anything – than nothing at all. So at the end of that first season, we were having Nando's brought into the dressing room after games. Nando's isn't that bad for you at all if you have the right things, but that was very much a short-term compromise before Mona arrived that summer to overhaul everything.

Now it's very different. With the new stand at Anfield, the dressing room is much bigger, with a full-blown kitchen next door, and the post-match spread is top-notch. Again, there will be everything – pasta, fish, steak however you want it cooked, salads, yogurts, fruit and so on. The food is varied and the menu changes every week. We'll have a protein smoothie prepared for our post-match recovery. It's measured out, depending on how long you've played. And unlike those shakes we used to have at Newcastle, they taste good.

Ultimately, nutrition is more about looking after your body for the longer term, so that you're able to recover properly between games and be in the best condition to perform week after week, month after month, year after year.

It's not just about keeping the weight off and keeping lean. It's about eating the right things at the right times in a schedule which, with all the travelling and late nights and different kick-off times, can be very irregular. If you don't refuel and recover properly, you'll find it hard to perform at your top level and there's more chance of getting injured because you're more fatigued. I'm sure some people will say, 'Come off it. People have always played every three days. They never needed nutritionists in the past.' Yes, but players are so much fitter now – partly because of nutrition and sports science and things like that. When the standards of professionalism are so high, it comes down to marginal gains. You need to break it down into the actual science of what the body is doing when you're running, say, 13 km in matches every few days – and with training and travelling on top of that. You can't afford to cut corners.

What do clubs make you eat diet-wise? Do you get cheat days? @Lynchyyy8

I eat very healthily, but I don't want to give the impression it's *all* steamed fish and protein shakes. I love a good roast dinner once in a while – roast lamb, mint sauce, Yorkshire pudding, veg and, as a proper northern boy, lots and lots of gravy. I love a nice burger when I'm on holiday. Not a McDonald's (which actually used to be a ritual of mine after the last game of the season) but a proper, nicely cut, nicely cooked burger. Where I go on holiday in Spain, they do a great burger with a fried egg on it, plus cheese, gherkin, proper salad, the works. Tempura prawns and mussels are other favourites when I'm on holiday. I don't mind ice cream. I don't mind the odd dessert. Favourite dessert? Apple crumble and custard. Solid, that, isn't it?

But those cheat days are rare. Ninety per cent of the time, I eat really healthily. As a professional sportsman, you just have to know when you can treat yourself and when you can't. In fact, that's the same for anyone. Even if you're a very healthy eater, you need your cheat days. I'll have a chocolate cookie now and then. It's just a case of knowing the right time for that.

Have you tried a roll and square sausage yet? @Jordan-Cowan4

Ha. You must be asking that because of that video I did with Robbo, who was talking about it like it was some kind of Scottish delicacy. The way he explained it, it sounded like a squashed hash brown. Maybe I should have had one when we were in Edinburgh in pre-season, but, no I can't say I'm desperate to give it a try. Sorry . . .

What made you decide not to touch alcohol? @ayamashalal

People talk about this like it's a big deal, but it was just a decision I made when I was young and I've stuck to it. To be honest, it was probably partly because, having broken into the first-team squad just before I turned 17, I was more conscious of my responsibilities – not just about alcohol but clubbing, nights out and so on. Around that time, a few of the YTS lads would go out into town with some of the older lads, like Matthew Kilgallon and Frazer Richardson. They would go into nightclubs and people would look at their faces and say: 'James Milner isn't here, is he?' It wasn't that I was a superstar or anything like that, but because I had got into the first team and scored a few goals, a lot of people in Leeds knew my name and the whole city knew I wasn't 18 yet. If it had got back to the manager, I would have got in real trouble. So even if I had wanted to go out drinking or clubbing, I couldn't have done. And around that time, I just made the decision that I wasn't going to. When you're younger, it's really just a question of whether you're comfortable in that scene. At that age, I wasn't.

You do have to make sacrifices when you're a professional footballer. The rewards are worth it. Is being teetotal really a sacrifice? I don't know because I've never tried alcohol. Well, I did have a sip of my old man's Strongbow when I was young, but that's it. From what I can remember, it didn't taste like it would be much of a sacrifice. The amount of time we spend away from home feels much more like a sacrifice to me, but it's also a case of not getting involved in things that your mates are doing when you're younger. You've got a choice to make. I always felt like I was happy to miss out on that side of things because I had a clear picture of what I could gain.

I do like a night out, though. I'm not a big fan of night-clubs, because I'm not a drinker and I'm not a smooth mover like Bobby Firmino or Crouchy, but I like going to bars and having a good crack with my mates. I don't mind people around me having a drink. It doesn't bother me at all. If other players like a drink, and that's their release, I'm absolutely fine with that.

The funny thing is when people say, 'Come on, just have one,' like they want to be the one who turns me, or they'll say, 'Please can I be there when you have your first drink?' Another line I've heard a lot is, 'Are you going to have a drink if we win the Premier League?' or 'Are you going to have a drink if we win the Champions League?' And in case you're wondering, no I didn't. I wasn't even slightly tempted. To be honest, I would have been more likely to turn to drink if we hadn't won it.

When on their end-of-season break, do most players have a fitness regime to keep themselves in shape? Or do they say, 'Stuff it, I'm on holiday'? @Skidz81202182

I don't think you can afford to think that way these days. The days of players putting their feet up for six weeks are long gone, which is why, a couple of weeks after winning the Champions League, I found myself running around the top of a mountain in Spain, in sweltering heat . . . and being attacked by a dog.

I have a place in Spain, where there are two options running-wise. One is a really long slog down to the beach and the other is really steep, ridiculously steep, running around the top of the mountain. The second is very quiet, with not many houses, so I prefer that one. I was running down from the top of the mountain and there were two women who had six or seven dogs with them. I tried to run around them and, as I did, one of these dogs went for me – actually tried to bite me on the knee – so I tried to hurdle the dog and, as I landed, I fell awkwardly onto the curb and took a tumble and scraped all down my arm. I had to carry on running because I was mid-interval at the time, but I met up with Adam Lallana the following day to play golf and he was saying, 'What the hell have you done to your arm?' It could have been serious, but Ads couldn't stop laughing when I was telling him about it. Neither could I, to be fair.

A footballer's summer is a lot shorter these days. This year we had the Champions League final on 1 June and then we were back in pre-season training on 6 July. That's five weeks. It was a lot less than that for those players who were on international duty, particularly the ones who were playing in the Copa América or the Africa Cup of Nations.

I enjoy my holidays – I went to America this summer, then to Spain – but I probably only allow myself to be in 'holiday mode' for the first week or ten days. And holiday mode, for me, just means taking it easy and doing things with the family, rather than eating or drinking loads. A lot of people will know what I mean if I say that going to Disney World with the kids isn't the most relaxing way to spend a holiday.

After a week or so, I feel ready to start running again anyway. But even if I didn't feel ready, the club gives us fitness programmes for when we're away. And our programmes are all linked to various apps, so the coaches can monitor what we're doing. Sometimes I'll do steady runs, but you don't often run at a steady pace as a footballer, so the steady stuff is just to build up your base fitness. After that, a lot of it is interval-based. I like to do four four-minute runs with a minute's rest between each one. Then it might be 45 seconds on, then a 15-second rest, in four-minute blocks. And when I say 'on', I mean running flat out.

One of the difficulties when you're on holiday is finding somewhere to do it. If you're on a beach, that's not easy. I used to run on a treadmill a lot in the summer. These days I prefer being out on the road – but ideally I'd prefer not to have dogs trying to get a piece of me.

Talking of dogs, there are stories about how, back in the day, fitness coaches used to give out heart-rate monitors so they could track what players were doing exercise-wise over the summer. Apparently some players used to put the monitors on their dogs and let the dog run around for an hour or so to make it look like they'd been running like mad.

You could never get away with a stunt like that these days. Everything is tracked in great detail. We also have to text the manager or the fitness coach to tell them we've done our sessions. He's a lot more hands-on than other managers. He always likes to be in contact with the players, particularly during international breaks, and to be made aware as early as possible if there are any problems. I just tend to text him, 'Session done.' He normally replies with the thumbs-up emoji – though this summer he responded with a few cowboy hats. I'm not entirely sure why. One time he messaged back with a picture of him in a hot tub. Maybe he was trying to tell me to relax.

I'm sure you could lie about your summer fitness work if

you wanted to, but you would only be kidding yourself if you turned up for pre-season out of condition. They just like to be kept in touch. They like you to let them know if the fitness work is going okay – or if there are any problems, like you've been attacked by a dog. Or bitten by a spider, like Robbo was.

What happens if you come back from pre-season overweight?

You're probably asking the wrong person. My biggest challenge over the summer is to avoid losing too much weight. This summer I lost 3.5 kg in the ten days after the Champions League final. We'd had various parties, late nights, not getting much sleep, not really eating properly, going on holiday, Disney World with the kids, playing golf, being on the go and then starting running again. I was burning a lot of calories, but not having a big breakfast, big lunch and big dinner like I do during the season. If I don't have three big meals, including a massive bowl of pasta, I get to the point where I'm losing weight and I think, 'Oh no, Mona is going to go mad at me.'

I was fine once I was back into my fitness programme and I was eating properly. When I came back for pre-season in early July, I was 0.5 kg off what I'd been at the end of last season. That's fine.

If you do report back overweight, you'll end up doing a lot more running on your own with the fitness coach, your diet will be monitored and you'll be weighed every day until you're back to your normal weight. Back in the day, players would train with bin bags under their kit to help them sweat the alcohol out of the system after a heavy night, but those days are gone really. At most of the clubs I've been at, the majority of the players are internationals and they're playing matches through half the summer anyway, so you only tend to get three or four weeks off, or five at the most, rather than the eight-week breaks that people used to have.

Is it true some players tried to report back for pre-season on a different day in order to avoid being humiliated on the lactate test by James Milner? @TakkiLFC

Haha. The lactate test is just one of the tests we do on our first day back. We get tested for absolutely everything – not just weight but body fat, which is tested in two different ways, then blood tests, heart scans, concussion tests, running tests, balance tests and so on. It's like a very detailed MOT, really. You're filmed running on a treadmill and they study your technique to see if there's any slight imbalance. The same with squats. If you're even marginally more comfortable on one side than the other, left or right, they'll build different exercises into your programme to balance that out and they'll review it again to check it's working. The attention to detail is massive.

The lactate test measures aerobic endurance, i.e. stamina.

You would be better off getting an explanation from a sports scientist, but basically it involves running laps of a 400-metre track – two, three or four laps, depending on the level – at a set speed, which increases with each level. After each level, blood samples are taken from your ear lobe to measure the amount of lactate your body is producing. Generally, the harder you find it to run at each speed, the more tired you will get, and this will be shown by the lactate that is accumulating in your blood. You keep going until either you're so exhausted that you can't keep up with the required speed or the fitness staff pull you out, so it's a test of physical endurance but also there's a mental endurance side to it too.

Joe Gomez does really well. Adam Lallana too. But everyone's fitness level is different. In certain positions, like central defence and centre-forward, you don't really need the same stamina levels and it might be more about sprinting. Bobby Firmino has fantastic stamina and does a lot of high-intensity running, but that's unusual for a centre-forward. Bobby is a machine.

Is it a motivation to be at the top for those fitness tests? Would you worry if your scores were down significantly from the previous season?

Yes, I would, definitely. My age gets brought up a lot these days – whether that's by the media or by my team-mates –

but I've come back for pre-season and managed to perform at the same levels as last year and I felt good doing it. It's important to me that I'm not dropping a level. That's not to say I'll be able to keep doing that for ever and be the same athlete, but every year that goes by, I feel good. If some of the lads are feeling the strain after a tough session and I feel all right, then I know I must be doing all right. I don't think there can be many managers who work their players harder in pre-season than ours does. If I can last the pace of a Jürgen Klopp pre-season at 33, that's a good sign.

I remember training on the beach on my second day of pre-season after joining Newcastle. They only had one fitness coach at the time, so he had one group doing a circuit while Gary Speed took another group of us running. Speedo was 34 at the time and he was still fit as anyone. If there are days when I feel a certain session is particularly tough and I ask the lads and they're saying, 'Yeah, it was really hard,' then that's fine. The day to worry will be if I'm blowing afterwards and they're saying, 'No, that was fine. What are you on about?' That will be, like, 'Uh oh. Is this the moment . . .?'

How do you split your days in the gym? @amarh7

I'll go into the gym every day. Some days it's just for pre-activation, which is a preliminary warm-up before we go outside. That's just a case of getting your glutes and the rest of your muscles warmed up, but it has become an important part of the training regime. Then a couple of times a week I'll do harder sessions before training – maybe 45 minutes on upper body and core – and a 45-minute leg-weight session when I can fit that in, which is usually a few days before a game.

You sometimes hear people say that players need to 'bulk up', but it's a fine balance. It's important to keep things ticking over, but I wouldn't want to get any bigger over the course of the season. I just want to be strong enough to make me a better player, which helps you when you're off-balance and things like that. It's more important to concentrate on your core strength and things like proprioception, which is working on your balance and coordination.

Football isn't like, say, golf, where you have a fixed position and you need to be strong in a certain action that you repeat again and again. In a contact sport, you're hardly ever in a fixed position. You're more likely to be off-balance or trying to hold someone off, so you need to have the core strength to be able to deal with that. It's also about building up the strength to try to avoid injuries and deal with the workload you need over the course of the season.

The sports science side helps a lot with all of that. They have all the data from the tests we do, so they know how much work each player needs to do over the course of a season to make sure we're strong enough but not too bulky. There was one stage when I was at Newcastle years ago where there was a lot of talk about how much we could all bench-press. You do need core strength, but as a footballer, it really isn't about how much you can lift. Let's be honest. That particular technique, lying on your back, lifting a bar bell, isn't very useful for playing football, is it?

Team-mates: Part One

Who is your favourite team-mate in each team you've played for and why? @jirayuketsuwan

It was strange at Leeds because I had my mates from the academy, like Scott Carson, and then, when I was 16, in the first few months of my YTS, I was fast-tracked into the first team and I didn't spend much time with them after that.

Alan Smith – Smudge – was probably the one I had most in common with. But that was pretty weird in itself because he had been my hero a couple of years earlier, when I had Leeds posters all over my wall, and now he was my mate. He was my favourite player – a local lad who had broken into the first team and done what we all wanted to do. He scored against Liverpool on his Premier League debut as an 18-year-old and then three days later he took a session with us as part of his coaching badges, which he was doing at the time. We were all, like, 'He just scored on his debut at Anfield, in front of the Kop, and now he's coaching us. This is amazing.' And then when I broke into the first team, he was the only one I really knew, so we became good mates and it eventually reached the stage where I stopped feeling like asking him for his autograph when we were out.

Smudge and I became closer when he joined Newcastle a few years after me. The girls got on well too, so the four of us met up most evenings. It was great having him at Newcastle. Steve Harper, a really nice guy, took me under his wing when I first went there and Shay Given, Alan Shearer, Andy O'Brien and Gary Speed were great too, but Smudge was the one I was closest to.

Another Leeds player who ended up at Newcastle with me was Mark Viduka. He was another one who looked after me. He used to call me 'Milli Vanilli' and he would insist on explaining it to me every single day. 'Do you know who Milli Vanilli were? They were this band in the eighties and they used to mime on stage and no one knew until the CD jammed and they got busted.' 'Yes, Viduks. You told me yesterday. And the day before . . .'

I had two spells at Aston Villa. When I first went there on loan, I was friendly with Aaron Hughes and Gavin McCann.

When I signed permanently, it was almost a whole new squad and I got on well with Gareth Barry, Stephen Warnock, Nicky Shorey and Luke Young. I see Warny a lot socially now – probably more than when we were playing together.

We had a good group at City. Joe Hart and I had been in the England squad together – under-21s and seniors – and we get on really well. I'd played with Gaz Barry at Villa and we got to know each other better at City. Both of us love golf, which helps. I sat next to Joleon Lescott in the dressing room and he was the first person I told that Amy was pregnant. Micah Richards was another who I'd been in the under-21s with. He's a brilliant lad, Meeks – a Leeds lad like me. He's so passionate, wears his heart on his sleeve, loved playing the game, incredible athlete, a gentle giant . . . until he lost his temper. When that happens, you need to be somewhere else.

When I came to Liverpool, I knew Kolo Touré from City and I knew Ads, Hendo, Studge and Clyney from England. But I like to remind Hendo that he barely spoke to me when I first arrived. Eventually I managed to grind him down, but I would still end up in his driveway or on his doorstep and not get invited in. It takes a long time to get close to Hendo. Ads says it was the same when he arrived, but the three of us are really good mates now along with Robbo, Trent and Ox. If that sounds like it's just the British lads sticking together, it's probably more down to the fact that we spend a lot of time playing cards or games on the bus and most of the other lads look at us wondering what on earth we're doing when someone gets their ears flicked for getting an answer wrong at *Tenable*. I think you can see from the way we play and celebrate together on the pitch that the whole squad is very together, regardless of where anyone is from.

I've often got on well with the staff at the clubs I've played for – not just the players. But it can be weird in football. You spend so much time with your team-mates, you know everything about each other and you go through so many ups and downs together, on the pitch and off the pitch, and then one of you moves on and you barely speak to them again. You want to stay in touch, but with the football schedule as full-on as it is, you don't really speak to them again. You might send them good luck messages and you'll have a brief chat if you're playing against them, but life moves on very quickly. It's sad, really, because often the wives and the families get to know each other too. Amy will see something on Facebook and she'll say, 'Oh my God. Remember so-and-so's baby? Look at them now. They're 12.' That's life these days, especially with men being so bad at keeping in touch. But I still speak to Harty all the time. We go back years, to when we were in the under-21s, and I'm sure we'll be mates for life.

Do you pick your room-mate for pre-season/away days or is it random to get the squad more integrated? @Bobbby-firmino

When it's the night before a match, during the season, we each have a room to ourselves. Given that the whole idea is about giving us the best opportunity to relax, without any distractions, that makes a lot of sense. It's not ideal if one of you is an early-riser and the other one likes a lie-in, or if one of you wants to sleep in the afternoon and the other doesn't, or you're on the phone, and so on.

We do share rooms when we go on team-building trips, though – like on our pre-season training camp in Evian. An important part of team bonding, or was it just because it was an expensive hotel on the shores of Lake Geneva? Who's to say?

I was with Robbo. As far as irritating habits are concerned, I pointed out to him on the second morning that he had been talking in his sleep – whispering something I couldn't make out. So that night we decided to use this sleep-talk-recording app. (Yes, such a thing does exist.) When we played it back the next morning, the first two recordings were of me. The first one, I was talking total gibberish in Spanish – 'Me dice . . . sabado . . .'. The second one was me saying 'Well done, that. Very well done.' The third one was Robbo letting out what sounded like a very loud moo. The whole thing was bizarre. Most unsettling.

Robbo should probably just be grateful that I didn't sleep-walk, like I occasionally do. There was one time when I was a kid and my grandma, who was looking after me, went to check if I was in bed. I wasn't there. She checked my sister's room. I wasn't there either. And she started worrying, looking all around the house. She got downstairs and I was sitting up, an inch from the TV, watching Nirvana in concert – totally out of it. There was another one where we were on holiday in the Maldives and I wasn't there when Amy woke up. She found me asleep on the bathroom floor. I was lucky. We were staying in a house on stilts. I could easily have wandered off into the sea.

Getting back to Robbo, he was no bother at all as a room-mate. He sleeps in longer than me in the mornings, so I had to be quiet. The first morning we were in Evian, my alarm went off, so I jumped out of bed to have a shower and . . . you know that thing sometimes when you get up too quickly and you feel faint? Well, that happened – not just my head feeling faint but my legs feeling like jelly, so I wiped out and fell across the room. I was just laughing to myself, thinking what would have happened if I'd stacked him or if he'd woken up to this massive crash. He slept through it all, though. I got up, still laughing, had my shower and, as usual, left him an abusive note on the shower screen so that he would see it later when it steamed up. All pretty grown-up stuff.

When I first started out at Leeds, it was always two to a

room. The first time I went away with the first team, my room-mate was Michael Bridges. His regular room-mate must have been injured. I was as nervous as hell, being away with a senior player. That wouldn't be allowed now as a 16-year-old, under safeguarding rules, but I was nervous simply because I was away with the first team and wondering what Bridgey and the rest of the senior players would think of me. I had only done my GCSEs a few months earlier.

Bridgey was good, though. I remember we all went to Harry Kewell's room to watch him and Michael Duberry play *Tiger Woods Golf*. They were taking it very seriously. When I first went to Newcastle, the younger players had room-mates but the senior guys didn't. Over time, it has become standard for players to have their own room.

Sharing can be a bit of a culture shock when you're used to having your own room, but it does bring you closer together, which is why we do it on those team-bonding trips. It's just important to give each other space. I roomed with Sadio on one trip and he was praying when I came back from breakfast, so I walked straight out again because I didn't want to disturb him or disrespect him. But it's great to be able to get to know your team-mates better.

The good thing about this Liverpool squad is that you could put me in a room with any one of those lads and it would be fine. There is honestly nobody in that dressing room that you couldn't get along with. I know we as foot-ballers always say that kind of thing in interviews – 'Yeah, we've got a great team spirit,' blah blah blah – and that hasn't always been true when I've said it, but it's true of Liverpool. It's rare. When you think of any workplace with 25–30 young lads, it takes some doing to create an environment where everyone respects each other and gets along. We've all had arguments on the pitch or things like that, but straight afterwards, it's always fine. I can't pretend that has been true of every team I've ever played in.

How similar or different is the public perception of footballers/ managers/pundits compared to the reality? @slightlycrunchy

That public image is often based on one incident or one snapshot of a person. People judge you on what they see on a pitch or from a five-minute TV interview, where you're trying to catch your breath and make sure you don't say anything that will get you in trouble, or they judge you on one single thing that they might have read about your private life – which might not have been true in the first place. You get pigeonholed. People make their minds up about you very quickly and they decide what they think you're like. Even if you're nothing like that, it's hard to shake off that label.

But even when you're a player yourself, you can sometimes form a completely wrong impression of another player. For years, I had a negative view of Gary Neville. I don't know whether it was just because I'm a Leeds fan and he's clearly Manchester United through and through, or whether

I made my mind up when I was playing against him, but I just assumed he was a total . . . you-know-what. And then I was in one England squad with him, towards the end of his career, and he was just hilarious: brilliant company, one of the funniest players I've met – and certainly the most surprising.

Sometimes you've just got to get to know someone better, like with Frank Lampard when he came to City. I had been in England squads with Frank Lampard for years, but I didn't really know him. It was only when he joined City that I really got to know what a great guy he is. That was the thing with England. You can meet up with the squad five times a year and be together for ten days at a time, but it never really felt in my time like many of us got to know each other all that well.

I can't say I got to know David Beckham well, but although he's fairly quiet and shy in some respects, he is every bit as classy as he probably comes across. It was quite intimidating for young players walking into that England squad when I did because there were a lot of big hitters – and none bigger than him – but Becks always went out of his way to talk to the younger players. I was playing wide at the time, so we would do crossing drills together. The way he delivered the ball was just *ridiculous*. He was a properly nice guy, a normal guy really.

While I was at City, we played a pre-season game against LA Galaxy when he was there. He came to our dressing room afterwards and gave signed shirts – personalised – to Harty, Gaz Barry and me. That was a really nice touch. He's clearly very aware of how famous he is, but not in an arrogant way. He's a nice, normal guy who happens to be incredibly famous. There was always a bit of a crowd whenever we went anywhere with England, but when Becks was there, that went through the roof. It was always very impressive the way he dealt with that fame. I don't think I would like it, but he always seemed comfortable with it. It never seemed to affect him.

How mad is Mario Balotelli? @dankiely

Mario isn't mad. He's a good guy and an incredibly talented player. The easiest way to describe him is to say that he was like a 12-year-old. That might sound like I'm digging him out, but I'm just trying to explain what he was like. He had this fantastic skillset and a great physique, but in other ways he was like a big kid who hadn't grown up. If a few of us were having a conversation and he was on the opposite side of the dressing room, he would make a loud noise or do something daft so that he would get attention. A lot of the things he did – like throwing darts, wearing that glove-style hat he had and even the car he drove with the camouflage wrap – seemed to be about trying to get attention. And whether that's out of insecurity or whether he had found it hard to grow up, because he had such a difficult upbringing, that's what he was like.

I had a few to-dos with Mario, which was usually if he was messing around in training and not taking it seriously. I would have a go at him, tell him to get his act together or whatever. But then he would always come up to me afterwards or the next morning and say, 'I'm sorry. You were right there. Fair enough.' And it takes a certain humility to do that. He was totally harmless and there was nothing malicious about him. He wasn't a bad guy at all. He just craved that attention. That's what some people are like.

And he made some huge contributions for City. I'll never forget his performance in that derby we won 6–1 at Old Trafford. That was the day that summed up the Mario enigma. The headlines that Sunday morning were about him causing a fire at his house by setting off a load of fireworks in his bathroom – probably because he was bored. It's not really what you want your centre-forward to be doing in the build-up to a massive game. There was a lot of focus on him that day ... and then he scored two great goals to put us on course for an incredible result. And he lifted up his shirt to reveal that T-shirt that said 'Why always me?' You couldn't help but laugh.

I wasn't laughing the time he drove his car into mine in the car park at Carrington, City's old training ground, mind you. It's not easy trying to get camouflage paint off your car. But you couldn't ever stay frustrated with him for long.

Do players take much notice and talk to each other about transfer rumours? @jaydorrian93

Not really. I don't take much notice. Sometimes you see a report and you think, 'Yeah, I could see that. That makes sense.' Other times you'll think, 'Well, I'll believe that when I see it.' It might sometimes crop up in conversation when two players are talking, but it's never a big issue. Liverpool are probably linked with 100 players in every transfer window. If you were going to take every one of those links at face value, you would drive yourself mad.

If you're at a big club, you know they'll always be interested in signing top-class players and there will always be competition for places. They know what they're doing and you let them get on with it. I wouldn't go asking the manager or the recruitment team about it. I want to be playing in the strongest team possible.

When the rumours are about yourself, that's not easy, but as a player you tend to have a pretty decent grasp of what's happening. When I was 18 Leeds sold me to Newcastle before I even had a chance to think about it, but these days it's much more rare for a deal to be done behind a player's back. Nothing happens overnight any more. When it's your own future, you try to block it out, like I did in my final year at City, but you know you're going to get asked about it, so I always made sure I had an answer in my head beforehand, just stating the very basic facts and saying that all I could do was concentrate on my football. That might sound very @BoringMilner, but it's the best way to act in that situation.

How much does positivity/negativity on social media really affect players? @tharlay9

More than it should, I would say. Football is hard enough with the various ups and downs you go through without being affected by social media, but it has become a massive thing in football now. When I first started playing, there wasn't any social media. If you had a poor game – or even if you didn't – you might get a bad write-up in the paper or the commentators might say something on the TV, but that was it. These days everything is all over social media and if a player looks at Twitter after a defeat, he's likely to have people all over the world hammering him for his performance or saying he's not good enough.

You can choose to pay attention to that or not. It's up to the individual. I think it's best to try to ignore it. Why would you go looking to see if people are hammering you? As with everything, it's important not to get too carried away when things are going well and not to get too down if things go badly. On social media, those ups and downs are going to be exaggerated after every result – good or bad. It's a lot harder to stay on an even keel if you're fixated on what people say on social media.

And what about the mainstream media?

You don't really hear players talk about the mainstream media as much these days, because so much of the focus is on social media. I don't read newspapers, to be honest. I'll flick through things online, just to see what's going on, but if someone has written that I've had a poor game, that doesn't interest me at all. That's just their opinion. My dad? That's a different matter. When I was very young, he would get very protective, saying to me, 'That guy is a such-and-such. Never do an article for him again.' I could understand him being protective. I wouldn't want anyone criticising my son or daughter either. But when it's about you, you have to be thick-skinned about it. Don't let it bother you.

They looked after me well media-wise at Leeds. I didn't do a lot of press at all for a long time at the start. They eased me in with Paul Dews, at the *Yorkshire Evening Post*, and John Bradley, who was Radio Aire and is now at LFC TV, who I still speak to now. They said they would look after me with those first interviews. Even if I had slipped up with them or said something stupid, there wouldn't have been a problem.

I've lightened up a lot media-wise over the last few years. I was a bit more defensive when I was younger. You become more comfortable with it over time. Most players would say that. Certain players refuse to do interviews. Ashley Cole was one. I don't think I would ever refuse. That's not to say that

I like doing it, but it's part of your job these days to speak up for your team when you're asked. I probably suffered for that when I was with England. It always felt like whenever there was a scandal or controversy, the FA's media guys would put me up in front of the cameras because they felt they could trust me to handle those situations without saying the wrong thing. I felt like a nightwatchman in cricket. It wasn't great fun, if I'm honest, just trying to straight-bat their questions away. I expect that's partly where the 'Boring Milner' image came from.

The only grievances I've ever had have been when something I've said has been twisted into a headline that suggests something completely different. When I signed for Liverpool, I said something totally straightforward about coming here and wanting to win trophies. That was twisted to make it look like I was having a pop at City and that I'd left them *because* I wanted to win trophies – which would have been a ridiculous thing to say, with the players they had and all the trophies they had won over the previous four years. I really wasn't having a go at City, but that's how it was presented and it inevitably got people's backs up. One City fan said to me on Twitter something like, 'You were a fan favourite here, but your comments since you left . . .' – and I just thought, 'But that's not what I said!' But that's the way it was reported and that's how it is remembered. You live and learn.

Footballers only seem to train for a couple of hours every day, so what do you do with all that downtime? Are you on the golf course every afternoon or, as it appears on Twitter, do footballers spend all their downtime in Nando's?

I would *love* it if we could spend every afternoon on the golf course, but that just isn't the case these days. At Liverpool, we're often training in the afternoons or evenings and we don't get many days off at all, so the amount of downtime isn't anything like what you might get at some clubs. And downtime means recovery time, when you're urged to relax and take things easy, so golf is generally off-limits anyway.

I play a lot of golf over the summer, but it's a real struggle to fit a round in during the season, particularly when you've got two matches a week. In the past it always used to be in club rules that if you were playing at 3pm on Saturday afternoon, you couldn't play golf beyond Wednesday afternoon. If you've got matches Saturday-Wednesday-Saturday-Wednesday, with European commitments, you can't really do it. If I'm able to get a round of golf in, it's usually during international breaks, now that I've retired from England duty.

Funnily enough, we used to play a bit on international breaks when we were away with England under Fabio Capello. He loved a round of golf. We would stay at the Grove, a big hotel in Hertfordshire with its own golf course, and because we were holed up there all week, Fabio would let us go out and have a round there. As a footballer, you wouldn't usually play golf on a Thursday ahead of a Saturday game, but we did that once and we won on the Saturday and, because Fabio was very superstitious, we always had to play nine holes on a Thursday from then on. That's quite a strange superstition, looking back.

I play off seven or eight. When I'm playing a lot in the summer, I can play pretty well, maybe three or four over, but during the season, it's hard. It's one of those games you need to play regularly. I do love it, though.

Do you play Fantasy Premier League with your team-mates?
@LukeLFC88

I don't these days, but I used to years and years ago. A few of the lads at Liverpool have teams. Robbo definitely does and I'm certain he picks himself – although, let's be honest, with all those clean sheets and assists, you probably would pick Robbo, wouldn't you? He might let you down on the goalscoring front, though. Maybe Trent would be a better pick . . .

I used to have a fantasy team when I was at Villa and I did pick myself at some point because I was playing well at the time. But we had a really good defence at Villa so I probably would have had to make that my priority, picking Richard Dunne, James Collins, Luke Young or someone like that rather than myself or Ashley Young. You know me. I would have done what was tactically right for the team – in true @BoringMilner fashion. I certainly wouldn't have been afraid of dropping myself, having a stern word with myself in the mirror.

This reminds me, actually. I used to play *Championship Manager* quite a lot. I played as Leeds when I was younger, but what I also liked doing was taking over Guiseley and trying to take them up from non-league. The best I ever did was getting them into the Champions League. They even expanded the stadium to 13,000 capacity, which, if you've seen Nethermoor Park, would be quite a transformation. I can't remember who I signed, but I was relying heavily on loans. I was ahead of my time, clearly.

But no matter how hard I tried, I could never manage to sign myself for Guiseley. I never had enough money to get as far as getting Leeds or Newcastle or whoever to accept an offer for me, never mind being able to offer myself personal terms. So instead I would just try to keep an eye on myself, check I was doing all right. I would make a comment about my pretend self in the pretend media every now and then, just to boost my morale. 'Praise James Milner's recent performances.' 'What are you doing, mate? Why are you talking about him? You're manager of Guiseley.'

It's funny with all these games, where they've rated every player in just about every category you can think of. There are so many categories and clearly it's just somebody's opinion, but you look at them and you think, 'Well, *that's* ridiculous, *that's* ridiculous. Oh, that one's higher than I was expecting, so maybe they *do* know what they're talking about . . .' Stamina was always my highest. I like to think there's a bit more to my game than just running up and down.

Sometimes you get asked to sign one of those cards of yourself, where, again, they've rated you in different categories. Someone asked me to sign one and I was, like, 'Pace . . . 63?! And have you seen what they've given me for passing? Do you realise I got most assists in the Champions League?' Before I signed it, I chucked it down as if I was genuinely angry about it. I hope they realised I was joking. I was quite pleased with 63 for pace, to be honest . . .

How do senior players let the manager know they don't rate the new multi-million-pound signing and he shouldn't be in the team? @nointent

I wouldn't dream of doing that. I've sometimes heard similar things about certain clubs in other countries, but I definitely couldn't imagine it happening at Liverpool. It will often take new signings a bit of time to get up to speed with the way we train and the way we play, which I know some players have found difficult at first because it's quite complex. But as a team-mate your responsibility is to try to help them with that, not go behind their back.

What you do get sometimes is mickey-taking. If someone

signs for big money and they shank it wide during a shooting session, you'll often hear, '*How* much?' That's good-natured, rather than malicious, but I'd say players are a lot more sensitive to new signings these days, particularly players who are coming from abroad. You don't just say things like that and expect them to know you mean it in a light-hearted way. It has changed, but I certainly got a fair bit when I signed for Newcastle, Villa and City. '*How* much?' It was great when I signed for Liverpool, because I was on a free transfer, so nobody could say it . . .

Is there much jealousy over wages? @gyna118

No one talks about wages, really. If they've got a contract negotiation coming up, they'll want to know what's realistic in relation to their team-mates. That's probably a normal scenario in all workplaces, but in football it's something most players would rather leave to their agents to sort out. There wouldn't be much point obsessing about one of your team-mates earning more money than you. That wouldn't be healthy. The one thing you might get is a few jokes, like if certain players get a tight hamstring, they'll be told they need to switch their wallet to their other pocket. But generally players don't talk about wages in the dressing room.

Training Ground: Match Preparation

What's a typical training day? What time do you start/ finish? @Shadows07847621

There isn't really a 'typical' day. Essentially, during the season, most teams operate on a loop, where you're always building up towards match day – except the day after a game, when it's a recovery session. Then, the day after that, you're building up towards match day again.

If I use the example of a week at Liverpool where we're playing, say, Saturday, then Tuesday night at home in the Champions League, then Saturday again, there's very little time between matches and the emphasis will just be on trying to keep us all in peak condition while making sure we're prepared tactically for the matches in question.

The morning after a game, we're always in for a recovery session. I'll normally eat breakfast at home, then get in for 9am and probably go straight into the treatment room so that the physios or masseurs can give me whatever I need recovery-wise or maintenance-wise to keep me going. I think most players would tell you they almost always have something that needs looking after. Very often when I'm playing, I'll pick up some kind of knock, or there will be some other ache or strain that will need to be managed over the course of the season. That's why those recovery sessions, the morning after a game, tend to be minimal in terms of how much you exert yourself. Some of the lads will have an ice bath, which helps muscles recover. Some will go on the bikes just to loosen their limbs, or they'll be in the pool. If you're out on the training pitch, it's usually just for a light jog – say two ten-minute runs – unless you weren't involved in the previous day's match, or you were only briefly involved as a substitute, in which case it will be your toughest session of the week.

A recovery day will also include a post-match debrief from the manager. He will have watched the match back by then, as well as getting all kinds of feedback from the video analysts and the data analysts, so that will be detailed – but because there's always another match just around the corner, it will always be geared towards the next match rather than the one that has just gone. The day after a match isn't the most strenuous. Years and years ago, it would have been a day off, but these days it makes sense for the players to use all the great facilities at the training ground, rather than just put our feet up at home.

If we're playing on the Tuesday evening, we'll usually train on Monday evening. Our manager is a big believer in linking training times to kick-off times. For years in this country we've been used to training in the mornings or at lunchtimes, but when you think about it, it doesn't make much sense to do that when your body is then expected to be in match mode at 8pm. Everything we do is based around kick-off times. It just makes it a bit frustrating when you have three games in a week, all kicking off at different times, which sends your schedule all over the place. It has been known for a player to turn up at completely the wrong time.

If it's a Tuesday game, having played at the weekend, then that Monday session is so important. We'll normally start with a passing drill, like a rondo, and then we'll do a lot more work around that particular game. We'll do 11 vs. 11, which normally gives you a pretty clear idea of what the team is going to be. One team will be the likely starting line-up and the other one will be set up like the team you're going to play the next day, whether that means defending in a certain way, getting the ball out to the wings quickly or whatever. We'll do drills to practise certain defensive or attacking movements, based on what we've been doing well or what we need to improve on, or based on what the coaches think can work against the team we're playing. If they've got a weakness at left-back, or if they're vulnerable to a certain kind of cross, then we work on that. If they're particularly strong in certain situations, we'll work to combat that. We also work on set-plays – attacking, defending, corners, free kicks – the day before a game.

If it's an evening match, we'll train the morning of the game too. If it's an away game, that will usually involve finding another club's training ground or a non-league ground and using their facilities. Again, it will be tailored towards the opposition, whether it's something tactical or set-plays or whatever.

By Wednesday morning, if we've played the night before, it's another recovery session and another debrief. Some teams will have a guaranteed day off every week, but we tend to come in most days unless the schedule is particularly quiet that week. It's hard to squeeze in a day off when we have a midweek game, but Thursday, two days after a game, might be a lighter session or a general football session – passing drills, rondos, etc. The day before a game, we'll always do older players against the younger players and the results will be totted up over the course of the season. Who usually wins? Let's just say there's no substitute for experience.

And then Friday is pre-match again. If it's an away game, we'll usually travel on Friday afternoon and stay in a hotel overnight.

If we do manage to get a day off in the week, there's always a double session the next day – morning and then afternoon. Our manager loves a double session. With a double session, we'll train late morning, then have lunch together at the training ground. If we've got time to kill before the afternoon session, a few of us might go for a coffee and then come back. The afternoon session is often a bit of a beasting – a really tough session. In one pre-season the gaffer had us doing triple sessions. Manuel Pellegrini liked to throw in the odd triple session at Manchester City too. It's pretty gruelling.

How many times on a training field have you spoken with a manager/coach and actually thought, 'Wow, I learnt something then'? And who was the coach/manager? @Dave_Tweets13

It probably doesn't happen as often as people would imagine. Once you're in the first-team squad, you're expected to know how to play football and instead the emphasis will be more on tactics and gameplans than on one-to-one coaching. Because I broke into the first team so early at Leeds, I remember Terry Venables saying to me, 'You're still going to have to do your technique work with the academy because you're not going to be able to get that when you're training with the first team.' So I was training with both. It was hard work, but it was important that I was able to do that.

I remember Terry giving me a good piece of technical advice. He talked about the number of times in youth football where you see a winger going towards the byline at pace and he tries to cross it to the far post and it just sails over the crossbar because he's off-balance. He said if I was in that position, running at pace towards the byline and looking to cross it, the best thing to do was to try to dink it to the edge of the box and, because you're stretching, with the angle of your foot, it's more likely to end up in the middle.

You don't generally get many tips as a professional footballer. It's not like golf or something like that, where you might modify your swing. In football, it's as if you're beyond that level when you're playing in the first team. You're expected to be at the required technical level already, but the best managers and the best coaches will still work on something with you in training or after training, or they'll show you videos.

I didn't work with Brendan Rodgers for long after I arrived at Liverpool, but he was one who would pull you aside and go through videos with you and things like that. The way his coaching sessions are structured was very good. It happens under Jürgen Klopp too, where he'll say, 'Right, we need to be better on the ball, so we're going to work on this.' That's massively important, particularly for the younger players, but I would say the overall emphasis at Liverpool is on doing things collectively. We have a particular style of play and we work very hard on different ways of defending and building up within that system. The improvements we've made over the past few years are there for all to see, so it clearly works.

How much work goes into improving specific skills – crossing, dribbling, shooting, etc?

As I said, the higher you go, there's an expectation that you're up to a certain level technically. It's not like academy level, where there's a lot of specific work on skills, but there are a lot of passing drills – rondos for example – and shooting drills, which are designed to improve your ability to play at a high tempo and produce quality in tight areas.

Beyond that, players will do different exercises on their own after the session has finished, working on their crossing or their finishing or whatever. There's the set-play work we all do together, where we're working on certain situations, and then other players will work specifically on dead-ball delivery, whether it's shooting free kicks, crossing free kicks from wide areas or whatever. I'll practise free kicks, but I don't often get to try my luck in games because Trent is all over them.

Trent's delivery is brilliant. He hasn't scored all that many free kicks at first-team level yet, but he certainly will do because his technique is so good. Harry Wilson is the same. They're two of the best I've played with. Ian Harte was amazing at Leeds. And of course there was David Beckham. Watching him in England training, his free kicks were just a joke. He was 34 by then and he was still working on his technique after nearly every session.

How much information are players given on opposition teams and specific players? @Enarrik

It varies from one manager to another. Some give a lot. Some don't give much. At Liverpool we'll have a video meeting the day before every game. The video analysts will work with the coaching staff on the presentation. One part of it will focus on the opposition, which means watching clips that show both their strengths and their weaknesses, and one part will focus on us, which means looking at things we need to do better but also looking at strengths that we can utilise against these opponents. It's broken down into how the opponents attack, how they defend, how they react in transition and so on. The manager and the staff will go into details about those weaknesses and how we're going to exploit them – and then, obviously, their strengths and how we're going to guard against them. If there's a particular type of attack that the coaches think can be effective against these opponents, like cutting back crosses towards the penalty spot, they'll show us clips of when that has worked well for us. We'll look at set-plays – free kicks, corners, the way they set up when defending, their movements at attacking corners – and again we'll go into detail about what their weaknesses are and how we're going to exploit them. Then we'll go outside and work on everything we've discussed.

Those video sessions happen before every game, but they will also e-mail us clips which will be more specific to us, recordings either of our own performances or of one of the players we're up against. Can they tell if we've watched them? I presume so, because we have to log in to watch them. I've heard stories about certain managers giving a player a blank memory stick – and then having their suspicions confirmed when the player in question claimed to have watched it. I can safely say our manager wouldn't need to have any concerns like that with this squad.

We're so much more aware of our opponents' strengths and weaknesses than we used to be when I started out. In those days you would get titbits that came from the scouts, but it would be things like 'so-and-so is vulnerable on his left side', 'so-and-so likes to check back onto his right foot'. It wouldn't be anything like as in-depth as what we get now, which can be a detailed breakdown of how the opposition like to press from the front and how we can play our way through it or around it.

The reality is that if you're competing in European competition as well, you don't get much time on the training pitch between games, so the information has to be spot on and delivered in a way that gives the players a clear sense of the gameplan. An exception would be, for example, in the build-up to the Champions League finals, where we had a lot more time to prepare and to think about individuals we were up against. Before the 2018 final we worked on a specific defensive plan for how to contain Cristiano Ronaldo, which I'd say we did pretty well. Even then, you don't want to go overboard with the video analysis. You've got to get the balance right.

At Liverpool, even though the approach is always about playing to our strengths, there are often little tweaks that are made with the opposition in mind. It might just be little things about how we build up from the back or slight changes to the way we press, but I think we've shown we can play with different formations and different systems even if the general principles remain the same. Sometimes things will be going so well that the manager will just want to keep things the same, but there are always a few tweaks made with the opposition in mind. I've played under some managers who haven't really done attention to detail, but you always feel more confident when you know the staff have done their homework and briefed you properly. There's always something there that you feel you can exploit.

What is it like working under Jürgen Klopp? @22nd_oclock

In one word: intense! Everything we do is intense. I've worked under a lot of managers and coaches in my career and his training sessions are more intense than under anyone else I've known.

He's a great manager. The best I've played under? Yes, I would say so. I'm sure it can be hard from the outside to work out exactly the difference that a manager makes, but if you look at the way our team at Liverpool has developed – the style of play, the way we defend, the consistency and, crucially, the way we've been able to play in that style, at pretty much the same level, even when we've had important players missing – that's a massive hats-off to the players but also the manager.

It's down to the way he prepares the team. Training is really hard. Really, really hard. And it's complicated. When we press as a team and we do it so effectively, we're not running around like a load of headless chickens. It's the result of a very specific gameplan that we've been working on for the past four years. When new players arrive, they often find it difficult at first to tune into that. It can take time to adjust to the intensity of the training session and to the tactical details, which are more complicated than people might imagine. You need to be so focused on the situation and on knowing that you are all where you need to be at all times, so that you can react to whatever situation arises on the pitch. People might imagine it's off the cuff – 'just go and press like crazy' – but it really isn't like that.

I don't know if there are other teams who work as hard in training as we do. Fair play to them if they do. Under our gaffer, there's never a single session where a player can switch off and just go through the session as if they're on auto-pilot. That can happen under some managers, because the intensity isn't there when you're training or because the sessions aren't demanding enough. But at Liverpool, it's intense and it's quite complex, so everyone has always got to be focused and plugged into it. If not, you'll mess up the whole session. And you don't want to get on the manager's wrong side . . .

I don't watch loads of German football, but I had watched the gaffer's Borussia Dortmund team in the Champions League and I had played against them for City. There was one Champions League group game when they came to the Etihad and absolutely battered us. We could have been 8–0 down – I'm not even exaggerating – but Joe Hart kept us in it with some incredible saves and we ended up drawing 1–1. Out of all the brilliant performances Harty produced for City, that one stands out. It was just insane. But I also distinctly remember us talking in the dressing room afterwards about how good Dortmund were. We were saying it was like playing against a swarm of bees – and not just because of their black and yellow kit.

That was the season that Dortmund got to the Champions League final, which obviously raised the manager's profile. People became a lot more aware of him and the way his team played. We saw the footage of him jumping around the touchline and the crazy side of him, so when Liverpool appointed him, I think most of the players were thinking, 'Could be interesting, this.'

Sometimes you think you've got an idea of what a manager might be like, based on what you see on TV and in the press and what you might have heard from other players in the game. They're not always how you think they'll be. Sometimes you're very pleasantly surprised by a manager. Other times you find yourself surprised in the opposite way. There are also some managers who are all charm in front of the cameras and totally different in front of the players.

With our manager, what you see is what you get. When he arrived, he said in a press conference that he was the 'normal one'. That really is what he's like. He's bubbly and he likes a joke. I'll never forget his team-talk the day of the Champions League final against Cristiano Ronaldo's Real Madrid in Kiev. There were a lot of nerves in the room, but then he started his meeting by showing us that he was wearing some CR7 boxer shorts. He had even tucked his shirt into them. We all cracked up and the laughter totally got rid of all the tension that was threatening to build up.

At the same time, though, he's extremely driven and serious about his work. You know where you stand with him. If you've got an opinion or concern about something, you can speak to him and he'll listen. He might well tell you to 'do one', but he will still listen and take on board what you've said. As an example, when he first arrived and he was trying to get us up to speed with his way of playing, he didn't give us any days off, which, with the number of games we had that season, with two long cup runs, was really tough. He changed that and now it's spot on. We still train very hard, but there's also a bit of downtime in the schedule. He's the one who makes the decisions, but he recognises the importance of listening to his staff and players too. He's good at that. Not all managers are.

Whenever a manager comes in, he needs to get his ideas across and his style across as quickly as possible. It's always going to be more intense at the start, when he's figuring the players out, testing their character, pushing them, challenging them, seeing what they're made of. The first session we had with our gaffer was during an international week. It was so physically intense, with so much sprinting and high-intensity running, that one of the young lads was sick at the side of the pitch.

He came down hard on us quite a few times at the start, but now, because the squad we have is so good and because he knows we'll put everything into every match and every training session, he rarely has to do that. He can be himself with us and joke with us away from the training pitch because he knows that when it's time to work, the boys will do that. With some squads, if they have a couple of players who might get a bit loose and fall into a false sense of security, a manager might have to worry about what kind of vibe he puts out. I think our gaffer has got us to the stage where he knows we'll be bang on it. It's very rare now that he has to come down hard on us. That's a credit to him and also a credit to the boys.

How can you play adeptly in different positions? Does it take any special training? @rifskysky

I played on the wing or up front when I was in the academy at Leeds. I was mostly on the wing when I broke into the first team and likewise when I moved to Newcastle and then Villa. I had barely played in central midfield much until my final season at Villa, but then Gareth Barry was sold to City and Martin O'Neill moved me into the middle alongside Stan Petrov. We didn't even have much of a conversation about it or do a lot of specific work on it in training, but credit to him for recognising that I had the right qualities and for giving me the confidence to believe I could do it.

It just seemed to click straight away. I got Young Player of the Year that season. I got the move to City and I got into the England squad – to play on the wing . . .

I always had it in mind that I wanted to move back into midfield, which was one of the attractions of moving to Liverpool. I played a lot more games in central midfield when I moved to Liverpool and I was enjoying it. Then, towards the end of the season, in the build-up to the away game against Manchester United in the Europa League, Alberto Moreno was struggling with an injury. We trained at Carrington, City's old training ground, on the morning of the game, and Albie wasn't fit, so the manager came over to me with a big smile and said, 'You've got a choice. Do you want to play left-back or right-back?' My reply was that this was like being asked which of the lads I wanted to let spend the night with my wife. At the time, the manager's English wasn't great – he had only been here for five months – so it probably went over his head. But I chose left-back. Despite being predominantly right-footed, I thought it would suit me more. On top of that, I thought there was no point asking Clyney to move to left-back so that I could replace him at right-back. My reasoning was that it was better to have one of us playing out of position than both of us. It went okay. We drew 1–1 and went through on aggregate. I think that persuaded the manager that I could do a reasonable job there in an emergency.

A few months later we were in Palo Alto, California, for our pre-season training camp when the gaffer asked if I could stay behind after a team meeting. It was one of those where the rest of the lads were looking at me as if to say, 'What the hell have you done wrong?' and probably wondering if someone had made an offer for me. They all shuffled out, looking back at me.

The gaffer told me he wanted to use me as a left-back in the season ahead. It wasn't something I was doing cartwheels about. I told him I really didn't see myself as a left-back. He kept saying he thought it was a good idea. Eventually I said that if this was going to work, they were going to have to train me up. They couldn't just expect me to make that adjustment overnight. I wasn't thrilled about it, but if this was the manager's decision, then I was going to have to throw everything into making it work.

I did quite a bit of work with the coaches in order to try to learn the position. There were specific things to consider on the defensive side, but also in terms of what you do in possession, because receiving the ball in the left-back position is very different from receiving it in midfield, where it's a lot more crowded. It's about learning how to use that space effectively. Also the physical demands are different. In midfield, you're up, down, up, down. At full-back you might not cover as much ground over the course of 90 minutes, but the distance you're running each time is higher and you might be flat out more, as you're making those runs to join the attack.

I know there's that thing about how you can't teach an old dog new tricks, but I think learning a new position is easier when you're more experienced and you're more aware, tactically, of situations within games and the positions you and your team-mates take up.

It's important that you think about the game, you have good tactical awareness and you have a good sense of what's going on. Then it's about whether you have the right tools to do it – physically, technically. Playing at full-back is a totally different discipline from playing in midfield. Defensively you're coming up against different wingers every week, which can be tough. Sometimes it will be a very tricky winger and sometimes it will be someone who's lightning-quick. Some like to go down the touchline and others like to cut inside. Your body position and defensive position have to change a lot from one week to the next, depending on what kind of player you're up against.

I'm comfortable with the ball on either foot. I favour my right foot, but it probably helps that I can use my left too. I prefer left-back to right-back. There are certain situations which are easier at right-back, like if I'm knocking the ball down the line or into the second striker, but at left-back it's easier to give my team-mates the eyes if I'm moving infield. People might think I'm always going to move inside from left-back, onto my right foot, but it totally depends on the situation. Our wide players, usually Mo and Sadio, tend to drift infield, so they're not always hugging the touchline. If there's no winger ahead of me, it's natural to check back inside anyway – the same as it would be for a left-footed left-back. If you can't make an easy pass because you're not comfortable on your left foot, that's an issue. But if you're comfortable with both feet and you're able to adjust to different situations, then it makes no real difference.

It's not easy, but it helps if you're fit enough to adjust, if you're comfortable on both feet and if you're the type of person who always wants to understand what's happening in every part of the team. Some forwards might switch off if the manager is talking to the defence and they feel it's not relevant to them – and vice-versa – but as a midfielder and a bit of a busybody, I always feel *everything* is relevant to me. I've also got the kind of stubborn character that wants to prove people wrong. When I first played at full-back, people were probably, like, 'James Milner at full-back? What the hell is going on here?' And I would want to prove them wrong. If someone thinks I can't do a particular job, I'll be even more determined to show them that I can.

I did pretty well there, I think, but the following summer I had another one-on-one chat with the manager – this time at my request. I told him I was willing to fill in at left-back whenever he needed me to, but, with Robbo arriving from Hull, I wanted the gaffer to consider me as a midfielder again. I knew that was a slight risk, because there was a lot of competition for places in midfield, but I needed him to know I wanted to play there. I was on the bench a lot at the start of that season and I hadn't played much at all by the middle of October, but I kept going, forced my way back in and ended up with nine assists in the Champions League, which was a record. I've still played left-back on occasions since, including in the second half when we beat Barcelona 4–0. I'm quite pleased with the way I've managed to add another string to my bow. I like to tell Robbo I've taught him everything I know about playing left-back.

You've played every position in your career except central defence and goalkeeper. Would you fancy giving those positions a go?

I did actually play centre-back in a pre-season friendly in Ireland when I was at City. I played as one of three centre-backs and then we switched to a flat back four. I quite enjoyed it actually, but it was a fairly slow game and our opponents weren't the best, so it was a bit different from being up against Cristiano Ronaldo or someone.

I wouldn't want to play there full-time, but it's quite nice when you're in possession and everything is in front of you. You've got at least half a pitch to play into. You've got your goalkeeper to go to if you're in trouble, but primarily everything is in front of you, whereas in midfield, things are going on to your left and your right and there might be someone pressing you from the front or from behind and you feel like you need eyes in the back of your head. If you're wide, you've got the touchline behind you and your options can be limited. Playing out from the back is a bit easier in that respect.

As for playing in goal, I've never done it in a game, but I used to love it as a kid, diving around. If ever Alisson got injured and we'd used all three subs, I think I would be the one rushing to pick up the gloves. I've seen Virgil have a go in goal, but I would be too worried about him getting injured, so I would insist it was me. I think most outfield players would secretly love to give it a go, but I would probably get bored after a while. Training always looks like fun for keepers, but in matches, there's a bit too much standing around for my liking.

When was the last time you bought your own pair of football boots? @TheSMorgan

Do you know what? I've never bought my own boots. My mum and dad always used to buy them for me. And then when I got into the England under-16 squad for the Victory Shield I was given a pair of bronzey, browny boots to wear by Nike. I remember finding it unbelievable that Nike wanted me to wear their boots and I didn't even have to pay for them. Not long after that, they offered me a contract. I found it hard to get my head around that at the time. 'Nike – *Nike* – are going to pay *me* to wear *their* boots?! And give me loads of other gear too?!' I was sitting down with the guy from Nike, gobsmacked, and he asked me if there was anything else I needed. The only thing I could think to say was that my flip-flops were a bit knackered and I could do with a new pair. The Nike guy laughed his head off. Most people asked for tracksuits, boots and trainers, all the latest gear, and I was asking for a pair of flip-flops. I probably missed a trick there – a bit of a schoolboy error, but in my defence I was a schoolboy at the time.

I've been with Nike ever since. At Premier League level,

most players will have a boot deal of some sort. When I was coming through, there was a scheme with the PFA, where one of the suppliers would provide players with two pairs of boots at the start of the season and a pair of trainers. Leeds were with Nike at the time, so everyone got a pair of boots and flip-flops if they didn't already have their own boot deal.

For a long time, I used to say I would never wear coloured boots. There were all these pink and luminous yellow boots coming into fashion when I was growing up. There would usually be only one player wearing them in each team. More often than not, he would be a bit of a show-pony, so I thought, 'No, that's not for me. I'll stick with black boots.' I swore I would stick with black, but then it reached the stage where, if you were wearing black, you would be the one who stood out because everyone else was wearing coloured boots. I was probably being stubborn at the end. There weren't really any black boots to choose from, so I had to take the plunge.

I actually quite like the coloured boots now. What I didn't like at first was that you would stand out if you were wearing blue or yellow or pink. But coloured boots are the norm now. If you have black boots now, you're most likely a referee.

Do you wear a different pair of boots every week? Tom Barwise

No. Some players do, but I like to wear them as long as possible. Nike generally change the Colorway range every three months and I'll have one or maybe two pairs in that time. If they get ripped, I'll need a new pair, but that doesn't tend to happen.

I tend to have two different pairs of boots on the go at once: one with six studs and the other with moulded studs. Moulds are comfier and I'll generally wear those every day in training unless it's slippy. You just can't afford to slip in a game, so I'll wear studs on match days. Some people like blades, but I've never worn them because if a blade gets caught in the ground, it can get stuck and it can cause you to injure your knee, whereas if it's round, it will rotate with you.

When I first started out at Leeds, one of the many YTS jobs was to wear the first-team players' boots in for them, so that they were broken in by the time they had to wear them. You would end up with blisters, but it was still amazing to think you were wearing a first-team player's boots. You don't need to do that these days because the boots are so much lighter and we're lucky enough to have them custom-made for us, so there's much less risk of getting blisters, but I will still look to wear them in gradually, rather than wear a new pair straight into a game. It's a case of picking the right training session to do that, which generally means a more low-key session – passing drills, maybe – rather than something full-on. That will be the only time I wear studs in training.

Nike are great. They don't just give you their boots to wear. They'll make whatever modifications you want. I've had a few foot injuries in the past, so they have produced a carbon plate for me to put in the bottom of the boot and make it more rigid. If it was too flexible, the foot wouldn't get enough support and it might lead to problems. A lot of players have different issues, which Nike will sort out. My left leg is ever so slightly longer than my right. That's quite common, but it could potentially cause an issue that would lead to injuries, so I have a tiny raise in my right boot. That attention to detail is designed to eliminate any potential problems.

The other thing I wear is an orthotic insole in both feet. It wouldn't be the right thing for every player, but I had a lot of pain in my fifth metatarsal at one point and I also had issues with my heel for a long time – the plantar fascia, which was agony. I broke my foot when I was playing for Newcastle at Anfield in 2008 and I had a few problems when I was coming back, so that's when I first started wearing an orthotic. It just slides into the boot to replace the normal insole. I definitely wouldn't recommend it for everyone, but it's what I've done for years and, touch wood, it has worked well.

There are other little things that Nike do. They put an extra hole in for my laces, so they don't gape. Any change you might want to make, no matter how small, they're willing to do it. Some people talk about boots as if the biggest thing is how they look, but by far the most important thing is comfort. The fact that they look great as well is a bonus.

What was your most embarrassing moment during a training session? @Lewis23890

I always try to crase embarrassing incidents from my memory. But your question reminds me of something else, which was the strangest incident I've ever witnessed during a training session. I'm not going to name the player, the manager or even which club I was with at the time, but a certain player had fallen out of favour with the manager and had been training with the reserves. The reserves trained in the mornings and the first team were training in the afternoon because it was the day before a game and we were going to travel straight to the hotel afterwards. We were doing 11 vs. 11 on the main training pitch, working on team shape, when suddenly this player drove his 4x4 onto the pitch and pulled up in the centre circle, mid-session, wound his window down and asked one of the other lads, who was his mate, what he fancied doing after the game on the Saturday night.

We were all just gobsmacked. The team-mate in question

just mumbled something back, clearly feeling incredibly awkward and embarrassed by the whole scene, wishing the ground would swallow him up. The manager was stunned into silence like the rest of us, not knowing what to say. The one who reacted was the assistant manager, who started screaming at the player to get off the pitch – pretty colourful language. With that, the player just finished his conversation and casually drove off the opposite end of the training pitch, over the next pitch and out of the training ground. None of us could believe what we had just seen, but we just had to get on with the session.

We don't hear much about anti-doping regulations in football – unlike a lot of other sports. Is doping taken seriously? What is the procedure?

I don't know about lower down, but certainly at the top level it's taken seriously. You get tested a lot – not just after games but also when the testers turn up at the training ground without warning.

It's not something you look forward to. You'll be out on the training pitch and you'll take a glance over and there'll be six people in blue bibs waiting on the touchline. And you hope it's not you that's picked, because it's such a hassle, but you recognise the importance of that process, so of course you go along with it.

The testers will pick a certain number of players to be

tested that day and one of the medical staff will generally come over during the session to inform those who have been picked. At that point, you start taking more water on board because it can be hard to provide a urine sample after a tough session – and particularly after a tough match – so you need to get plenty of fluid inside you. But there's a limit to how much you're allowed to drink because if there's too much water in the urine sample, they can't get an accurate reading.

Once the training session or the match is over, you leave the pitch with the testers straight away – no questions asked. You can't go to the dressing room, even if the manager wants to speak to you. You go straight in, sign the declaration forms and basically you have to stay with the testers until you're able to go to the toilet.

It's easier after a training session because, generally speaking, you haven't been flat out for long. When it's a post-match urine test, particularly in the heat, where you've lost a lot of fluid, it can take hours and hours to produce a sample. After Champions League matches away from home, where you're often flying back straight after the game, the players who are being tested generally have to make their own way to the airport after the rest of the team have gone. Then the sample gets sent off to the labs for analysis and, assuming all is fine, you don't hear anything else about it.

You have to be careful, though. There are a lot of medications that we can't take because there's a danger they might contain something that's on the banned list. If we've got a sore throat or a headache, we're advised not to take Lemsip or Nurofen because they might contain traces of certain substances that are potentially said to be performance-enhancing. As a general rule, we're told not to take anything unless it has come directly from the club doctor. If I buy medication from a chemist, yes it will probably be fine, but if it has been mixed in a factory where they have other substances, which might be on the banned list, I could end up with traces of that banned substance in my sample. If that happened, I would end up banned. Any medication the club medical staff gives you has always been batch-tested, which means there's a guarantee that it doesn't contain anything that shouldn't be in it.

It's not just after matches and training sessions that we're tested. They have the 'whereabouts test'. If you're not at training on a particular day – whether you're ill or you've got a scan or it's just a day off – you have to be able to give them a certain hour in the day when you can guarantee you will be at home or at a certain location, where they can come and test you. If you're not there when you say you're going to be, you get a strike. If you get three strikes, you're banned. If you refuse a test, you're banned.

I know people say the testing isn't as rigorous as in other sports, but certainly at the highest level, it would be very difficult to imagine anyone taking performance-enhancing drugs and getting away with it. The testing process feels constant. I doubt there are many players in the Premier League who don't get tested at least three or four times in a season. If you're playing Champions League or Europa League, it's a lot more. The clubs take blood samples regularly as well, testing for illnesses or abnormalities, so I really don't see how anyone could get away with taking something performance-enhancing.

Highs and Lows

In 2003 Peter Reid helped his old pal Andy King out by sending you down to third-tier Swindon on a month's loan. What are your memories of that spell? @LoathedStrangers

My first memory of Swindon is nothing to do with football. It's the famous 'magic roundabout' – the one with five mini-roundabouts on it. As a 17-year-old who had only passed his driving test a few months earlier, I found that terrifying. My first thought was, 'What the hell do I do here?' Basically, I ended up shutting my eyes and hoping for the best.

I did okay at Swindon. I played six games and scored two goals. It was a bit of an eye-opener – lads bringing their own pasta to eat on the bus, one lad getting caught in traffic on the way to a game and having to run the last mile to the ground – but it was a good experience. I wasn't really there long enough to forge any real friendships, but it was a great squad, with good pros like Sam Parkin, Andy Gurney and Sammy Igoe, and I was very grateful to their masseur, Trev Giles, who invited me to live with his family for the month because he thought a 17-year-old shouldn't be stuck in a hotel on his own.

When I got back to Leeds, Peter Reid said to me, 'Brilliant. That has made you as a player.' I think he wasn't sure about me beforehand, because I was only 17, and he saw it as a way to help out his mate Andy King, who is sadly no longer with us. I presume he got positive reports from Andy, which probably did 'make' me as a player in his eyes. I had already played half a season in Leeds' first team, so I hadn't been that thrilled about going on loan at first, but it was a good experience.

Is professional football as much fun as when you're a kid or does the business side take over? And: fans hate to see their favourites leave a club. What is it like being the player?
@Jonathan_Izett

There's no way it can be as much fun as when you're playing as a kid, simply because the day-to-day, week-to-week pressures are so great. You can still enjoy training and enjoy playing, but it's important to remember that it's your job and that you're playing for the supporters and for the club, not for yourself. That was pretty clear when I broke through at Leeds. Normally a young player would just be encouraged to enjoy himself when he breaks into the first team at 16 or 17, but Leeds were going through a very difficult period at the time, fighting against relegation, so, while it was an incredible honour for me to be playing for my hometown club at that age, I don't think I could really say it was always 'fun'. It was enjoyable when we were winning matches, but that didn't happen anything like often enough.

As a player, you don't really think about the business side, as you called it. But the moment I really became aware of it – the moment I lost my innocence, if you could call it that – was when Leeds sold me to Newcastle. And that also applies to the second part of your question. I'm not saying I was the fans' favourite, but they liked having local lads in the team and they always seemed to appreciate my efforts at what was a really difficult time for the club. I'm sure the fans were upset when I was sold. To be honest, so was I.

I'm still not sure how it happened. I was only 18 and I didn't have a clue how things worked or what was going on. Leeds had been relegated, which I was gutted about, and a couple of my team-mates had been sold at the start of the summer – Paul Robinson to Tottenham, Alan Smith to Manchester United – to try to ease the club's serious financial problems. But I was only thinking about Leeds and looking forward to trying to get us back into the Premier

League. I went on holiday and didn't hear from anyone at the club. There had been some talk about them extending my contract and, as far as I was concerned, there was not even a question of me leaving.

The first I heard of it was when I went in on the first day of pre-season training and someone said to me, 'Are you ready to go up to Newcastle tomorrow for your medical?' Hang on, what? That was genuinely the first I had heard of it. It was just really strange. Then I spoke to the club and spoke to my agent and, yes, Newcastle had come in and made Leeds an offer – £3.6 million rising to £5 million, I think it was. And Leeds had accepted it.

I said, 'Well, what if I don't want to go?' And the response from the club was along the lines of, 'We're really struggling for money. It would really help the club if you went.' And that was pretty much that. I was owed a signing-on fee from my contract and I waived that, again to help the club, because they really were struggling financially at the time. I did the first day of pre-season at Leeds and all these new players had come in, like Michael Ricketts, a lot of changes, and then I went up to Newcastle for my medical the next day and that was it. If it sounds like I was reluctant to leave, that was no reflection on Newcastle, which was a great club for me to go to – Sir Bobby Robson in charge, a team with players like Alan Shearer, Jonathan Woodgate, Gary Speed, Shay Given, Laurent Robert, Kieron Dyer, Craig Bellamy. It was just that I didn't really want to leave Leeds and the whole thing happened in a bit of a blur. It was the best thing for Leeds, but it just felt like I didn't have a choice in the matter.

You hear a lot about 'player power' and players forcing their way out of clubs and so on, but there are a lot of instances where players don't really have a say.

What was Sir Bobby Robson like to play for?

Unfortunately I only had a few weeks with him after I joined Newcastle. I was shocked when he lost his job four games into the new season. I didn't have anything like long enough with him, but he was out on the training pitch every day at 71, leading the sessions, and he was clearly still a top-class coach.

The biggest impression he made on me in that short time was through his personality rather than his coaching. He wasn't there for the first couple of days after I signed, but then on the third day he turned up and bounded over to a group of us and was rubbing his hands, saying, 'Right, where's the new lad? Where is he?' And I was *right* in front of him. He had this lovely air about him. There was a railway line that went alongside the training pitch and he always used to break off, mid-session, and wave every time a certain train went past. And he had this rule where, after training, everyone had to eat together and no one could leave until the last person had finished. And the last person to finish was always . . . Sir Bobby. He would walk in after everyone else had started and then he would have soup, main course, dessert, coffee . . . He was very traditional in that respect, but he was a top-class coach and a lovely fella and it was a sad, sad day when he left.

What did you think of Graeme Souness's unkind comment –
'You will not win anything with a team of James Milners'?
@WiseWallsender

At the time, as a young lad under a new manager at a new club, it came as a bit of a shock. It was my first season at Newcastle. Sir Bobby, who had signed me, had been sacked soon after I arrived and I was trying to establish myself at a big club, in a dressing room full of big personalities. For the manager to say that in a press conference . . . I'll be honest, it was a kick in the teeth at what was already a difficult time.

For an experienced manager, he didn't deal with it well. I was on the back of the bus and he called me to the front. It wasn't a discreet word away from everyone else. I was left standing up in the aisle with all the other players and staff watching. He said he had been misquoted and that he was just making a general comment about needing experienced players, rather than young players. There wasn't really much I could say in the circumstances, so I just mumbled something and sat back down again.

If anything, it drove me on. I didn't find it easy in that first season at Newcastle, and when he then sent me on loan to Villa, I was determined to prove him wrong, which I think I did. It was his opinion at the time and one that I wanted to change.

I have no problem whatsoever with Graeme. It probably got to him more than it got to me. He has mentioned it on several occasions since – both in interviews and when I've seen him. When we won the league the first time with City in 2012, he was on the pitch, for Sky, and he pulled me aside during the lap of honour and said, 'I never meant that the way it sounded, you know. I'm buzzing to see you win this.' I like Graeme. He's a legend of the game and I can get on board with about 90 per cent of what he says in his punditry. He's quite ruthless, quite old-school, but I like that.

Which transfer in your career was the most difficult to deal with personally and can you explain why that was the case?

The hardest one to deal with was probably the one that didn't happen. Newcastle had sent me on loan to Villa in 2005–6 as part of the deal to sign Nolberto Solano. Again, I didn't have much say in that. But the move went really well and the following summer I felt that, if I wasn't going to play much at Newcastle under Glenn Roeder, I would be interested in joining Villa permanently.

As is often the way with these things, it dragged on

towards transfer deadline day before Newcastle accepted a bid. I drove down from Newcastle to sign for Villa, but when I pulled up outside and got out of the car, Martin O'Neill came over and said, 'They've pulled the plug.' I initially thought he was joking. I didn't know him – he had just taken over from David O'Leary at Villa – but he said no, Newcastle had changed their mind and they were refusing to sell. I couldn't believe it. I was in Martin's office, raging about the situation. Martin said I might as well do the medical and sign the forms anyway, just in case Newcastle agreed to it. Rather than wait around, I drove to my parents' place in Leeds and watched the end of transfer deadline day on Sky Sports News, still hoping there would be some kind of breakthrough and the deal could go ahead. You know that feeling when you're watching deadline day and your heart is telling you there's still a chance a certain deal will go through but your head is telling you it's pretty much over? Well, that was me on deadline day that year. The deal didn't happen. Newcastle had been trying to sign Mark Viduka from Middlesbrough, but that had fallen through, so they had pulled the plug on my deal.

I really did feel like I was in limbo after that because I went away with England under-21s and I wasn't back at Newcastle until the following week. At that point, Glenn Roeder said to me, 'This is great. I never wanted you to go anyway. You're part of my plans.' Great, I thought. That was exactly what I wanted to hear. But then Saturday came and we were playing at home to Fulham and I wasn't even on the bench. It was the angriest I have ever been with a manager. I went into my office and said a few things I shouldn't have done. I was fuming. It's the only time I've been like that in my career and it was simply because it was ridiculous for them to pull the plug on the deal and then for me not even to be on the bench. After that, I got my head down and grafted and managed to force my way back into the team. I had a good season actually and scored quite a few goals, but it left a sour taste and I think those two deals – the one when Leeds sold me and the one where Newcastle refused to sell me – opened my eyes to certain things about the football industry. It can be ruthless and, although people talk about the players calling the shots, the reality is often the exact opposite.

One thing that has always bugged me is the role of an agent. How much of a role does an agent have in a player's day-to-day life? @renrocket07

I can see why you would ask this. Agents can get a bad reputation – deservedly so in some cases, I expect – but I've been with my agent, Matthew Buck from the PFA, for almost my entire career and he has been a great support in many areas.

The football industry is a minefield. It's different from other businesses. You can be a good businessman but it doesn't mean you'll know or understand the football industry. The contractual side is completely different. When I was a 16-year-old, breaking into the first team at Leeds, my parents and I didn't know where to start. No matter how switched on you or your parents might be, negotiating a contract with a football club is not something you're likely to be comfortable doing without professional help.

Knowing what I've learned by this stage of my career, I'm reasonably confident I could negotiate a contract, but it's not something I would want to be involved in. Contract negotiations are complicated and, even with the best agent, talks can drag on for months. Things can get messy. If you were negotiating your own contract, you would have to go in and talk yourself up, which is not really something I would want to have to do. Players don't want to have to deal with meetings dragging on for months, where their value to the club is being debated. If there are difficult negotiations going on, you don't want that to be hanging over you as you train and play. I trust Matthew to look after that side of things.

I've read about some agents taking huge sums in commission from transfers – whether that's from the player or the club – but the sums the PFA take are much, much smaller and, in any case, they go back into the game, for example to the PFA's benevolent fund for players who have fallen on hard times. That's one of the great benefits of being with the PFA.

It's not just negotiating contracts. There are so many other things that an agent does – working with the club on commercial issues, negotiating with sponsors, dealing with the media, helping with a lot of other things that I do away from the pitch. When we set up my foundation, Matthew did all the work for that and he has remained very heavily involved with it.

We meet up regularly to discuss plans for the foundation. I know the perception of agents is a negative one, but I can only speak from my own experience with Matthew. He cares about his players and puts their interests first. He's someone I can totally trust, which means I can focus on what I do on the pitch.

Martin O'Neill divides opinion among Villa's fans. What did you make of him as a manager?

I thought he did a great job for Villa and a brilliant job for me as a player. I liked him. He was full of praise and warmth when you were doing a good job for the team. He could be pretty brutal if you weren't playing well, but some of the things he said made me laugh. There was one game where we were well off the pace and he said to Gaz Barry, 'You're everywhere, son – everywhere the ball has just been.' After another game, the TV cameras appeared to pick up Nicky Shorey calling him a w*****. Martin said to him, 'I've been called a w***** by a lot better players than you, son.'

He passed Luke Young in the corridor at the end of his first season. 'How would you say you've done this season, Luke?' 'Yeah, all right, boss. Pretty solid, I think.' Martin paused. 'Shall we say . . . adequate?' And then walked off.

His methods could be quite old-school. Steve Walford would take most of the training sessions and it would mostly be quite basic and off the cuff – small-sided games, the kind of things players enjoy. John Robertson would call you over for a chat and he would breathe cigarette smoke all over you, but the things he would say would make you feel ten feet tall. If you were playing well for Martin O'Neill, you would get so much praise and so much confidence. If you weren't doing it, that was a different story. We didn't see eye to eye when I told him I wanted to join City, but he was one of the managers I really enjoyed playing for.

What was your proudest and most memorable moment as a Villa player? @WFAPEX

I really enjoyed my time there. It felt like the club was going places. We got a good team together – solid defence, a good midfield and a lot of pace and quality going forward. I improved a lot as a player at Villa and I got into the England squad. I'll always be grateful for the opportunity Martin O'Neill and the club gave me.

That final season I was there, we were going for the top four in the Premier League and we were doing well in the

FA Cup and the League Cup. Beating Blackburn over two legs in a topsy-turvy League Cup semi-final tie was one of my best memories there. We won the first leg 1–0 at Ewood Park, with me scoring the only goal, and then we quickly fell 2–0 down in the second leg at Villa Park. Warny pulled a goal back and I then scored a penalty to make it 2–2 on the night and put us back ahead on aggregate. That felt like one of the most pressurised penalties I had taken. It ended up 6–4 on the night, 7–4 on aggregate, and it was a great atmosphere. The club hadn't won anything for a while, so it really did feel like we were on the verge of doing something special when we reached the final.

It was a very proud moment walking out at Wembley for the final against Manchester United. We believed in ourselves and we made the perfect start when I scored a penalty to put us 1–0 up very early on. Walking back to the halfway line, hearing the roar from the Villa fans, 1–0 up in a major final, that was a special moment. We just wanted to finish the job.

Unfortunately we lost the game 2–1 and that leaves a sour taste because, as every Villa fan will remember, United should have had Nemanja Vidić sent off for the foul that led to the penalty. It was a clear red card and it felt as if the referee decided not to give it just because it was a cup final. I think that was a game-changing decision. It still disappoints me when I think about it.

It just felt as if we hit a wall after that. A lot of us had played a lot of games that season. Squad-wise we were maybe one or two players short. It felt like we were very close with Villa, but we just fell a little bit short and it wasn't really clear whether there was going to be enough investment to help us make the next step.

Can you remember your last game for Villa? It was West Ham at home and you destroyed them single-handed. What motivated you to play that well when you were leaving? @knightrider1172

Yes, I remember it well. I like to think I don't need any extra motivation, but to be honest, one of the things that drove me on in that game was the thought that it could be my last game for Villa. Some of the Villa Park crowd were booing me at the start of the game, because they knew I wanted to leave, so maybe that drove me on as well.

There had been a lot of speculation about City all through the summer. I respected Randy Lerner, who was a really good guy, and Martin O'Neill, and I obviously respected the club, my team-mates and the fans, but I was very aware of City's interest. Everyone knew how ambitious City were and what they were trying to create, so of course I was tempted.

I had already told Villa that I wanted to speak to City if possible, but a deal hadn't been agreed. Then Martin O'Neill resigned just before the season started. Kevin Blackwell was put in charge and he said to me, 'Do you want to play?' I said, 'Of course I want to play. I'm still an Aston Villa player.' I was getting booed at first, but then I think the fans quickly worked out that, even if it was my last game, I was committed to Villa as long as I was wearing a claret and blue shirt. I was running around like an idiot, flying into tackles. I scored a goal and I think they could see I was still giving everything for the cause. In the end I got taken off with a few minutes left and I got a standing ovation. I appreciated that and it was nice that I was able to have that last game. If I'd been sold the previous day, or if I'd said I didn't want to play in that game, the Villa fans would probably have thought less of me. It was nice that I could show them my appreciation too. Often in football you don't get that opportunity. It was a great family club and I enjoyed every minute of my time there – both spells.

How was life at Man City and what was it like being part of their transition? @Chris_Cadaret

That was a big part of what attracted me to City in the first place – wanting to be part of something new and exciting. A lot was made of the money that they were spending at the time, but the people at the club had a clear vision of what they wanted to do. Lots of clubs spend big in the hope of winning something, but what really impressed me was a strong sense of what they were building. They made me feel it would be very exciting to be involved with that.

And it really was. I had never won a trophy with Leeds, Newcastle or Villa. At City I won everything there is to win in English football. I had five great years there. We won the FA Cup in my first season, which was the club's first trophy in 35 years and the start of that new era that we had all been talking about. Then a year later we beat Manchester United to the Premier League title with the final kick of the final game. That was unbelievable. We won another Premier League title two years later and the League Cup as well. The victory parades we had, going through the middle of Manchester, were fantastic. You could see what it meant to those fans and to everyone at the club after so many years without winning anything.

It was incredible to be a part of that era. It's strange that people seem to imagine I've got an axe to grind with City since I moved to Liverpool. I've got nothing of the sort. I loved being there. I played with some amazing players, like Vinny Kompany, Sergio Agüero and David Silva, who is a lovely guy and an absolutely incredible player to play alongside. I loved my time there, became a better player, won trophies and had a fantastic relationship with the fans and with everyone at the club. I made some great friends. I'm so grateful to have been part of that. It was a really special time for the club and for everyone involved.

Talk me through the final moments of that game against QPR when City won the league for the first time in 44 years.
Sam Jones

I was on the bench and for a long time it felt like it was turning into one of the worst afternoons of my career. We were 2–1 down, playing badly. The manager was going mad at the players and we knew Man Utd were winning at Sunderland. Ninety minutes were up and, on the bench, we thought we had blown it, which was a horrible feeling after we had played so well all season to put ourselves in that position.

After Edin scored in stoppage time to make it 2–2, we thought there was a slim chance. After that, we were all just standing up on the back row of the bench. Then the ball went down that end again, Mario knocked it through to Sergio – and everyone knows what happened next. As it hit the net, all of us from the bench sprinted onto the pitch and the celebrations are just a blur. It was an incredible moment. I can't even tell you where I ran to. I just remember mobbing Sergio. There was a pitch invasion at the final whistle and we had to run to the dressing room, where we were all in complete disbelief, thinking, 'Oh my God. What the *hell* just happened?'

Even now, I find it unbelievable, the way it happened. If it was a film where a team had gone so long without winning the league, and then to do it with two goals in stoppage time, to beat their fiercest rivals to the title, you would just say, 'Nah, that's just stupid. That wouldn't happen.' But it did. And it was one of the most amazing moments in football history.

When you're thinking about great moments from your career, do you remember them as they happened to you at the time or do you just visualise the TV highlights?

If it's a moment or goal I've seen a lot of times, it's probably a combination of the two. With, say, the goal for Leeds against Chelsea, I can still see it the way I did at the time, curling it into the far corner, and obviously I've seen the TV footage too. But also, because it's something my family talk about a lot and because I know Elland Road so well, I feel like I can also see it from where my dad was sitting and where Amy was sitting. I've sat in both of those places, so I can imagine what they saw – the goal and then the pile-on afterwards.

With the Agüero goal against QPR, I must have seen the replay a thousand times, but in my mind's eye I still see it as I watched it from the bench – Mario, off-balance, knocking the ball to Sergio, one touch to steady himself, BANG! And then complete bedlam.

The Champions League final is a lot more recent and a lot fresher in my mind, so I just remember Divock's goal as I saw it at the time. I had taken the corner from the right and I ended up near the corner of the penalty area, heading back to cover in case the shot was saved and Spurs broke forward on the counter-attack. I've seen clips of the goal many times, so I'm sure that, as time goes on, I'll think of the TV footage too. But it's always nice to remember moments like that the way you saw them at the time.

Champions League or World Cup. Which is the pinnacle of the game?

That is a really tough question. Historically it has always been the World Cup, hasn't it? But these days, with the best players from all over the world playing for the best teams in the Champions League, it feels like that is where you see the highest quality.

It was an incredible honour to go to two World Cups with England – in South Africa in 2010 and Brazil four years later – even if I barely kicked a ball in 2014. Particularly with the first one, everything about the build-up felt like it was going to be the ultimate.

But they both ended in real disappointment and I don't look back on the experiences with any real fondness at all. That is always going to be dictated by results to a large extent, so the whole thing was . . . bittersweet, really.

I had always wanted to play in the World Cup and I was delighted to force my way into Fabio Capello's squad, because I had only made my debut nine months earlier, having won a record number of caps at under-21 level. So I was buzzing. I've heard some of the lads say they didn't like where we stayed in South Africa, but I was buzzing just to be there. And I play golf, so it was fine by me. The facilities, the training and everything else was good. But the week before our opening game, against the USA, I fell ill with a stomach bug. I barely left my room that week and I lost a lot of weight. I felt like I was dying. There's no way I should have played, but Fabio had a team in his mind and that wasn't going to change, so I started the game and I ended up getting brought off after half an hour. It then became clear I wasn't going to start the second game, even though I was fit by then, so I was thinking, 'Bloody hell. If that's the only involvement I ever have in a World Cup – subbed after half an hour, feeling sick – not great, is it?'

We drew the first two games, against the USA and Algeria. We didn't play well at all, and we were getting hammered for our performances because all the talk from the media beforehand had been about how easy the group was. In the third game, against Slovenia, the pressure was really on us – we had to win – and that is probably my favourite World Cup memory because I put in a really good cross for Jermain Defoe to score the winning goal. To do that and play well in a high-pressure game was massive for me on a personal level, especially after what happened in the first game. But then we played Germany in the next round, which I'm still sore about.

As for my second World Cup, in Brazil in 2014, it really did feel like it was over before it began. We were knocked out after two games and I didn't play in either of them. I played in the third game, against Costa Rica, but that was a dead rubber.

In fact, my main memory of that World Cup was when Phil Jagielka and I were left fearing for our lives. There was a golf course right next to our hotel in Rio, so about eight of us went out to play one afternoon after training. It was getting dark and some of the lads had finished their round, so they left and got a lift back. Jags and I thought we would just finish the last two holes. When we finished, it was pitch black, but we could see the hotel and we thought that, because it was just around the corner, we would go through this gate. The gate swung shut behind us, so we started walking towards the hotel and, as we did, we became aware of these guys clocking us. They started shouting at us. We ignored them and carried on walking. Then they started walking after us. Then they started jogging. Uh oh. We started jogging. Then they started running towards us and we were, like, 'RUNNNN!' We were sprinting down this road, thinking, 'We're going to get done in here.' Then all of a sudden this Mercedes van pulled up alongside us, the door opened and we were thinking, 'Oh my God, this is it. We're going to be abducted. It's happening. We're screwed.'

But when the door opened, we saw it was the other lads, who had gone back to the clubhouse, with security, got in this van and were on the way back when they saw us running away from these guys. 'Quick! Get in!' So we piled in, with the van on the move, and we got back to the hotel. I don't think I've ever been so scared in my life. As for Jags, he's a lot quicker than people might imagine, but I've never seen him run that fast before.

If you had the chance to go back in time and replay one match from your career (not one moment – the whole match), what match would it be and why? @DickoLCFC

It depends what you mean by 'replay'. If you mean the chance to relive that game and experience it all for a second time, then I would say either Liverpool 4 Barcelona 0, which was absolutely incredible, or, because it's so long ago, my home debut at Elland Road, when I scored against Chelsea. That was nearly 17 years ago, and although in one sense it feels like it was yesterday, I'm sure there are parts of it that I have forgotten. If I could relive that game and just take in my surroundings and the atmosphere a bit more, that would be special.

But if you mean the chance to revisit a certain game and rewrite history, I would probably go for England 1 Germany 4 at the 2010 World Cup. There are others too – and I probably would have said the Champions League final against Real Madrid in 2018, had we not gone on to win it the following year – but that England–Germany one really sticks in the mind because it was a terrible scoreline yet we were left thinking about what might have been.

We started the game really badly and we were 2–0 down, but then we pulled it back with a goal from Matt Upson and then a minute later, as you might remember, Lamps struck a 25-yard shot that hit the underside of the crossbar, bounced down beyond the goal-line and then bounced out again. But whether it was the referee or the linesman who should have seen it, or both, it wasn't given. We couldn't believe it. Even from where I was on the pitch, pretty much level with the ref, it was clear it had gone in. It wasn't even close. It was about a yard over the line.

It was said to be the goal that prompted FIFA to bring in goal-line technology years later, but that was a bit too late for us. We thought we had scored two goals in a minute to go from 2–0 down to 2–2. We would have had all the momentum going into half-time, against a very young German team who were clearly rocking once we pulled a goal back. Might they have crumbled if that goal had stood? Might we have gone on to win the game and reach the World Cup quarter-finals? We'll never know, but it certainly felt like the momentum was with us at that point. But then they had that let-off and, instead of being in control, we were left to chase the game in the second half. We ended up being done on the counter-attack and losing 4–1. It went down as a real low point for England. Even though we didn't do ourselves justice over the four games, I've often looked back at that one and thought, 'If they'd had goal-line technology back then – or even just if the referee and linesman had seen it, like pretty much everyone else in the stadium did – that could have been so different.' And we had a good team at that tournament. We all know what football is like and how matches can swing on big decisions like that. That would have been a totally different game if it had been given, but instead we had to fly back from South Africa the next day to face the music.

What was the toughest moment or choice of your career?
@Ahardyz

Leaving City. Leaving Leeds at 18 was very difficult too, after they were relegated, but that wasn't my choice, whereas leaving City was my decision. They offered me a contract, I turned it down and I joined Liverpool. The attraction of moving to Liverpool was obvious, but to do that, I had to leave City, which wasn't an easy thing to do.

I had been at City five years, the longest I had been at any club. I had won lots of trophies and had a great relationship with my team-mates, everyone at the club and particularly the fans. It's hard to walk away from that.

There were various elements to the decision. One of them was timing. City were very good at tying down their players to long contracts and, if it was a player they wanted to keep, making sure they didn't get down to the final couple of years. By the start of the 2013/14 season, I was one of the only first-team regulars who was down to the final two years. I was really keen to extend my contract. I was playing a lot at the start of that season and, if they had offered me a new deal then, it would have been signed and sealed straight away.

But they didn't offer me anything at that time and, by the time we started talking properly, around February or March 2014, I wasn't starting anywhere near as regularly. I ended up only starting 21 games in all competitions that season, so that made me question whether committing to a long-term deal would be the right thing to do. They did make me an offer towards the end of that season, but I didn't feel I wanted to commit to it at that time. I turned it down. That's what tends to happen in contract negotiations. They're rarely straightforward, which is why I felt concerned that the club had waited so long to get started.

Nothing was sorted out that summer and then it ended up dragging on and on. I was just trying to keep my head down. Again, I was playing a lot during the first half of the season and playing well. The fans were amazing with me, singing my name, urging the club to 'sign him up'. That made the decision even harder. I didn't really know what to do, so I just focused on my football and told the club I would make a decision at the end of the season.

I was playing with quite a bad knee injury at the time, which, looking back, was a stupid thing for me to do because if I'd done any serious damage, I would have had no contract and no security whatsoever. I understand why some City fans are unhappy that I went on a free transfer, but I kept playing through the injury, with my contract ticking down, because the club came first. That was my commitment to City when I signed a five-year contract with them.

It was a really tough decision to leave. I would have been very happy to stay, playing for a great club that was competing for trophies. I was settled in terms of the environment. What unsettled me was the feeling that I wasn't going to play as many games as I wanted to and, if I was going to play, it seemed likely to be out wide, rather than in central midfield where I wanted to play. They ended up signing Kevin De Bruyne and Raheem Sterling that summer and I think they would have done that even if I had stayed, so it wasn't really clear where, at 29, I was going to fit into their plans. The way the contract negotiations went – or didn't go – probably reinforced that feeling.

Right at the end of the season, the chairman, Khaldoon Al Mubarak, made it clear that if it was about money, they would find a way to keep me. But it wasn't about money. By then, I felt ready for a new challenge. Liverpool came in for me at the end of the season and the project there appealed to me in the same way that the project at City had done five years earlier. When I went to City they hadn't won anything for a long time and one of the things that really appealed to me was the chance to be part of that revolution. That's how Liverpool sold it too: the chance to be part of a new era at the club. They saw me as one of the players who would help them start to win trophies again. That fitted really well with what I wanted to do. It was a risk, a challenge, but I've never been the type to shy away from that.

Ask the snake why he celebrated wildly when he scored for Liverpool against City, yet chose not to celebrate when he scored for City against Villa, saying it was out of respect for his former club. City and the fans were nothing but good to you, so why the inconsistency? @dave_bones

Snake?! A bit harsh . . . Okay. Honest answer. If you watch the footage again, as it sounds like you have, you'll see that I immediately stopped because I didn't want to celebrate – out of respect. And then I remembered there had been this agreement among a few of us that the next time we scored, we were going to do some daft 'cowboy' celebration, which was a joke that had come up when we were playing cards. I probably wasn't expecting that to happen against City, but it did. So, having not celebrated at first, I looked up, saw my team-mates, remembered the promise and then did this lasso gesture very quickly before stopping. I don't think I celebrated wildly, as you put it. I couldn't even tell you what was going through my mind at the time, but there was also a release of frustration, because City had beaten us in the League Cup final a few days earlier. I think I felt I had managed to strike the right balance between respecting City – which I do, massively – and keeping a promise to my team-mates at Liverpool.

I know a lot of City fans probably thought I should have toned it down, like I did when I scored a penalty at the Etihad the following season. With the one at Anfield, I thought I did tone it down. If it hadn't been against City, I would have done a lot more. Because it was City, it was just a very quick lasso thing and then I stopped – the bare minimum, out of respect. It's not like I ran around the stadium and did a knee slide. I do respect City and their fans enormously after the five years I had there, but some of their fans have held it against me. That's a shame, but I understand it. It was hardly an Emmanuel Adebayor, though, was it?

What was the reasoning for retiring from England so soon? Do you have any regrets and were you ever approached by Southgate? @Liam_Charley

No regrets. I was 30 when I retired from international football after Euro 2016. I had won 61 caps at senior level and, if I'm honest about it, the last few years weren't really very enjoyable. I wasn't starting games regularly and I felt that, rather than keep going away with England, I would be better off focusing all my attention on Liverpool and, of course, on a young family.

I had started games regularly under Roy Hodgson, but

then I seemed to fall out of favour. I was barely involved in the World Cup in Brazil in 2014 and then, with Euro 2016, I really might as well not have been there. I came on for the final minutes of our first game, against Russia, and watched the rest of the tournament from the bench. I felt I could have done a good job in midfield. I'd had a strong season at Liverpool, set up a lot of goals, got to the Europa League final. I was doing well in training and I wasn't getting a look-in. I can hardly remember a thing about that tournament now. I must have tried to erase it from my mind.

Someone said to me at the time, 'Don't get frustrated. You know it's going to happen, so there's no point getting frustrated by it.' That was good advice and it did help me to keep it in context, but it was still frustrating and I knew that, once the tournament was over, I would have to have a conversation about it. I didn't see the point in staying in the squad if it was just to make up the numbers, particularly if that was at the expense of a younger player who might benefit more from the experience.

When Sam Allardyce took over from Roy after the Euros, he came to see me and I told him how I felt. I like Sam a lot – he impressed me when I worked under him at Newcastle – and we had a decent chat, but my mind was pretty much made up and it felt as if he was fine with that. We put out a statement that I was retiring from international football and it was all as amicable and professional as it sounded.

Then, as everyone knows, Sam lost his job after one game in charge and was replaced by Gareth Southgate, who called me soon afterwards to see if I would reconsider. That was actually a more positive conversation than the one I had with Sam. Gareth was more enthusiastic about what I might bring to the team if I came back. If we'd had that conversation straight after the Euros, maybe he could have talked me out of retiring. But realistically, having made my decision, I wasn't going to go back on it one match later. My reasoning was still the same and nothing had changed. I had committed to my decision, for the benefit of my club career and the benefit of my family, and that was that.

Match Day: Pre-match

How do you travel to matches? Do you all go together or do you go separately in your individual cars?

If it's a home match, we always make sure our cars are parked at Anfield for us to drive home afterwards. Depending on the kick-off time, we'll drive to Anfield at some point – lunchtime if it's an evening kick-off, the day before if it's an earlier kick-off – leave our cars there and the bus will pick us up to take us to the hotel, where we'll have our pre-match meal. We'll then get the bus to the stadium so that we arrive about two hours before kick-off. We often get a big crowd gathering outside the hotel to wave us off.

Then the fans will line the streets around Anfield and wave their flags and sing their songs when we arrive. Especially for the bigger games, that really gets you in the mood.

If it's an away game, it depends how far we're travelling. If we're playing down south, we'll get the bus or the train down or we'll sometimes fly. Even if we've got the bus or train there, we'll usually fly back afterwards because you don't want to be getting back home at 10pm from a 3pm kick-off.

Back in the early days of my career, you weren't allowed your phone on the bus. These days most of the lads are on their phones or their iPads, listening to music, watching TV, playing games, on social media, messaging friends or whatever. A group of us will sometimes play cards or we'll play a game together on the iPad, passing it backwards and forwards to answer questions.

Another thing that has changed is the buses themselves. At Liverpool, ours has a full working kitchen on board and our chef travels with us to prepare our meals. It means that, rather than wait around to eat after the game, we can have our post-match meal on the way home – or on the way to the airport. Again, it's about minimising travel time and allowing the recovery to start almost as soon as the game is over. The days of pulling over for fish and chips on the way home are long gone.

Some things don't change, though. Whichever club you're at, everyone has their own seat on the bus. If you're a new signing or a young player, the worst thing you can possibly do – criminal, in the eyes of some – is to sit in someone else's seat. You've got to wait to see what seat is free. That has been one of the great dressing room laws for as long as I've been playing.

Do you prefer to stay in a hotel the night before a home match? @Walshy1664

Always, yes. Even when we're given permission to stay at home, like before an evening kick-off at Anfield, I tend to book myself into a hotel anyway. I got used to that when I was at Villa and City, where the whole squad would stay away before every game.

At Liverpool the plan changes depending on the kick-off time. Most games we go to a hotel, but if we're not playing until 8pm the following day, like a Champions League game or a midweek game in the Premier League, the club are happy for us to stay at home and then we'll meet up for training in the morning. But I just book myself into a hotel so I can get a good night's sleep and then wake up the next day with a routine I'm used to, with no distractions whatsoever.

It's another night away from the family, which is not ideal because you want to spend as much time with them as you can, but this is what works best for me in terms of focusing on the game. I wouldn't want to focus 100 per cent on the game, thinking about it every second of the day, because that would drive you mad, but I feel that doing this helps me to be free of other distractions. I don't have to think about anything else. It's a routine that has worked well for me for the past 12 years or so and I'll keep doing it, for however long I keep playing, because it's what works best for me.

How do you prepare on match days nutrition-wise as well as with sleep and daily activities? @amarh7

Sleeping patterns vary a lot, depending on kick-off times. If it's a 12.30pm kick-off, you need to be up and about early and you need to have your big pre-match meal around 9am, which isn't ideal. Whatever the kick-off time, we tend to get up quite early. Sometimes we'll go for a walk on the morning of the game to loosen our limbs and also just to get us out of the hotel. If it's a night game, we'll train in the morning and then maybe try to grab an hour of sleep during the afternoon. That has changed over the years. I went through a phase of never sleeping during the day ahead of a night game, but these days I always try to get my head down for an hour or so.

Whatever the kick-off time, we have our meal three-and-a-half hours beforehand. The difficulty there is that if you're a sub, you might not be playing until five hours later – or possibly not at all. You'll try to eat normally and then, before the game, maybe have some nuts or a cereal bar – something like that to tide you over.

The range of options at mealtimes is amazing. Ten years ago, it would just be pretty standard. Most players would have beans on toast, egg on toast, chicken, pasta, whatever. Now there's everything you can think of – well, no, everything healthy and nutritious that you can think of. There's cereal, chicken, fish, rice, pasta, salads – and the chefs will prepare it however you want, as long as it's healthy.

Everyone is different, though. Some players have allergies and can't eat certain things. One of the lads at Liverpool finds it really difficult to eat before a game. He'll eat the bare minimum at the pre-match meal. That's not ideal from a nutrition point of view, but it's a case of finding what works for you. We've all got different nutrition plans, tailored to what works best for each of us.

What's in the bag you carry off the bus? @Alex_Lanyon

I would love to be able to tell you there was something exotic or mysterious in there, but it's just toiletries. Deodorant, toothbrush, toothpaste, shaver, shaving foam, razor and hair wax. It's only a small bag. Nothing else would go in there.

Can players wear contact lenses when they play? @Alia-Liverpool

Yes. It doesn't seem to do Robbo any harm. But I had another team-mate at Manchester City who started wearing contact lenses and had to stop. He said that when the ball was coming over, he could see it too well. He could see precisely how it was spinning and it put him off, so he would miscontrol it. He felt he was better off without them.

It's match day at Anfield, an hour before kick-off. Please could you give us an insight into the mood in the dressing room. And how does the pre-match scene compare to when you made your Premier League debut for Leeds back in 2002? Simon Hughes

It's very different now. There was a lot more noise in those days. A lot more banter and a lot more shouting. These days most of the lads are on their phones, a lot of them with headphones on, and it feels a lot more chilled out. When I first started playing, there were no phones allowed on the bus or in the dressing room. I tend not to have my phone in the dressing room, but most of the lads do. Can you imagine if a manager banned phones from the bus or the dressing room now? There would be outrage. It's what relaxes people and helps them get ready for the game, so you wouldn't want to interfere with it.

We have a playlist where everyone chooses a song. Hendo takes care of that. That will change over the course of the season, but we try to have a range of music. There's some Latino stuff, some hardcore rap, a bit of African music. Sadio's music goes down well in the dressing room. Some of the lads will have headphones on anyway, listening to their own music, but the playlist is nice because it enables everyone to feel part of it.

We'll all get changed in our own time. Everyone has their own routine. Some will be reading the match programme. Some will be on their phone. Some will be silent, saying a prayer. Others will be having massages or getting strapped up or having a shower. There will be massage tables set up in the corner. Some dressing rooms are small so you can only fit one or two massage tables in there, but they'll put them in the shower area if need be. It's hard to imagine a pre-match build-up without people getting massaged, but if I think back to breaking through at Leeds, if I had got on the massage table for a rub, people would have been asking, 'What's going on here? Who does this kid think he is?'

I might be wrong, but I can't really remember us having music in the dressing room in those days at Leeds. There were nothing like as many of us. These days you've got at least 18 players, usually one or two more with the squad in case of injury, and the staff numbers are much bigger. Some of the dressing rooms really aren't big enough. Manchester

United actually made their away dressing room smaller last season. It's not about luxury. It's about size. It can be a real squeeze at some grounds for the away team, which I don't think is right when you consider the resources that Premier League clubs have. You need somewhere for pre-activation, which is the exercises to loosen you up before you do the warm-up on the pitch – stretching, warming up your ankles and your muscles, things like that.

About 35 or 40 minutes before kick-off, we'll go out for the warm-up, which is mostly about doing bits of ball work and getting used to the pitch and the conditions. We'll start by doing some basic ball work, just to get a feel for the ball and for the pitch. Then we'll do more some warm-up movements and stretching, then we'll do some long strides across the width of the pitch, then a passing drill, then a possession drill, which is usually four against four with the centre-backs at either end. (The subs do their own separate warm-up.) Then we'll do a shooting drill, followed by some sprinting, and make sure we're ready to go at kick-off time. We'll come back in together about ten minutes before kick-off – and at that point there are about seven or eight minutes before the bell goes. Some players like to change their boots between the warm-up and the game. Others need to get taped up or put their shin pads on.

The tone is a lot more serious at that point, a lot less laid-back. Different managers have different approaches, but generally you've had your main team-talk before then. A lot of managers will do it at mealtime at the hotel or before you go out for the warm-up. If there's a team-talk just before kick-off, it's usually a short, sharp message. Some managers don't say anything at all once they're at the ground. In those final minutes before you go out onto the pitch, there will be a lot of players going around wishing each other good luck.

The final thing before we go out is that one of the masseurs will put on another tune to get us fired up. The main one we had last season was 'All of the Lights'. It gets us going and there are a lot of shouts of encouragement as it builds up. Then we go out for the game together.

Do players get a say on tactics?

No. The manager and his staff are in charge. You can talk to our manager and express an opinion – that's not the case with every manager – but you're not going to say, 'Gaffer, we need to go three at the back on Saturday' or anything like that. They spend their time analysing and they know what they're doing.

As a senior player, you're more likely to have the kind of relationship where you can go to the touchline during a game and say, 'This guy is getting in behind us because of this' or 'This could be a problem,' or point out something that's happening at set-pieces that might be hard to see from the bench. But he and his staff will almost certainly have seen it anyway.

In certain other sports, like cricket, the captain plays a hugely important role as a sort of strategist, but in football it's not always obvious why it matters what the captain does. What qualities does a good captain need to have and who are the best captains you have played alongside?

One of the best I've played with was Dom Matteo at Leeds. He and the other senior players really looked after me and showed the importance of having good standards and a good mentality. He had a lot of injuries but was always willing to put his body on the line for the team. When a captain puts himself out there, even when he's carrying an injury, and the rest of the boys can see that what he's putting himself through for the good of the team, the natural thing to think is, 'If he's doing that, I'm going to do it as well.' Martin Laursen at Villa was similar in respect. Vinny Kompany was a brilliant captain at City – really well organised, got on well with everybody, led by example on and off the pitch, great at looking after the boys. If things needed to be said to the manager, he was great at that too.

Every captain is different. Some are loud. Some don't say anything on the pitch. Some don't even say much in the dressing room, but they lead by example. And it's not just on-pitch leadership. The captain needs to think about the whole team – not just collectively but the different individual characters within the team and what makes them all tick. If a player isn't pulling his weight and needs to be dragged into line, a good captain will try to do that without the manager or the coaching staff having to get involved. He will also try to smooth out any tensions between the players so that things don't get out of hand. Or if there's a player who's frustrated because he's not getting picked, or going through a difficult time away from the pitch, again the captain can show leadership to help with that. Hendo is great at all of that. He always puts the team first.

I'm not saying the captaincy is as important as it is in cricket, but it is important that you have players who can show leadership. There are so many things that people won't think of. Sometimes it's about going to the club and the manager and getting things organised, making sure everything is right for the players in terms of travel arrangements or training schedules.

As vice-captain, I'm involved in quite a lot of that at Liverpool. On the pitch, it's like I'm the good cop and Hendo is the bad cop. He'll give people an earful – whether it's his team-mates or the referee – whereas I'll be a bit more encouraging. Off the pitch, our roles are reversed and I'm the bad cop. I'll be moaning that things aren't right and Hendo will be the one trying to compromise.

Being captain isn't an easy job. I'm sure that for a manager, if you've got a good captain, like Hendo, it must be a huge benefit. The manager has enough to worry about. If he knows he can rely on the dressing room – that the team spirit is there, standards are high and the players are committed to doing the things he wants to put in place –that's a huge weight off his mind.

What kind of coin is used in the toss-up at the start? I've always wondered. @DJeanChurch

It varies. Most refs use a normal coin, but in the Champions League the UEFA refs have a special disc. One side is red and the other side is blue.

I actually got hammered on social media because of this. We were playing Red Star away in the Champions League and I was captain. They were playing in red and we were playing in purple. The atmosphere was one of the most hostile I've known. We were getting spat on as we walked out of the tunnel. Everyone was yelling at us and there was an incredible noise. There were red flares going off. The whole place: red. We went over for the toss. The referee got the disc out and asked me which colour. I said blue because at that time, it felt like red was the colour of the enemy. We were wearing purple, which . . . well, it's not blue, but it's close to it.

Apparently it got caught on camera and people on social media were saying, 'Why the hell has he said blue? Blue is Everton. We're Liverpool. We're red.'

I got hammered for it. All I can say is that if you were standing where I was at that particular moment in time, in the middle of the pitch, surrounded by red flares, red smoke, playing against Red Star, who wear red, you would understand why I didn't say red.

This Is Your Captain Speaking

FOUR QUESTIONS FROM JORDAN HENDERSON . . .

In the dressing room before games, we have tunes playing which have been picked by all the players. Can you please tell your readers which song you picked and why? And if I'm allowed a follow-up question, if the music wasn't for a football dressing room environment and trying to get revved up for the match, which tune and artist would you pick. (PS – if you don't pick a Westlife track, you're lying . . .)

Wasn't my choice 'All of the Lights'? That's hardly Westlife. We ended up having that as our walkout tune last season, just before we went out onto the pitch, so it can't have been a bad choice, can it? I like a bit of Chris Brown, a bit of Ed Sheeran, but I'll listen to absolutely anything. And Hendo knows as well as I do that all the lads like a good singalong to Westlife.

I've already mentioned the brilliant playlist that Hendo does for the dressing room before matches, where we each choose a song. Usually it's more upbeat stuff, but there was one pre-season game this year where for some reason we decided to go very cheesy on the bus back to the hotel and we had all sorts – Janet Jackson, Mariah Carey, all that sort of thing – and we were all singing along. Possibly a bit of Westlife too.

You once famously said you would never use social media and you've even more famously changed your mind – so much so that you're now the king of Twitter and Instagram. You've never given me a good explanation for what changed your mind, so now is the time. Do we have to thank the @BoringMilner parody account for flushing you out?

Partly because I wanted to keep track of what you lot were up to!

And also because I wanted to follow your amazing picture captions: 'Good performance and 3 points', 'Preparations for tomorrow's game', 'Working hard at training'. I might have to start a @BoringHenderson account, you know . . .

Ten years ago, when a player walked into a dressing room, everyone would be bantering away. These days a lot of the banter is around social media, and I wasn't involved in that at all, so it was partly to get involved – not just with you and the rest of the lads but to engage with the fans a bit more and maybe give a bit more of myself.

The @BoringMilner thing never bothered me. I don't mind if people think my life revolves around ironing, drinking tea and clearing out my sock drawer. I actually thought for a while that one of the physios at City must have been behind it because some of the jokes were a bit too close to the truth. The only things that annoyed me even slightly were being asked about it every time I did an interview, and the amount of traction it was getting. @BoringMilner had 20 times more followers than my foundation, which . . . okay, I get that, because it's quite funny at times, but it just felt like there was more I could do to push the foundation while also engaging with the fans and the lads a bit more. And instead of doing that, I had left a gap. So in the end I felt like there were more pros than cons and I decided to go for it.

I had always been quite private and I just felt it was probably time to start giving people a bit more of me. Not too much – I don't do anything involving my family because I believe there are certain parts of my life that are private – but just enough to let people know what I'm about and what I'm thinking and to laugh at myself a bit. Social media is strange, though. I'll tweet something important about the foundation and it will get hardly any likes. Then I'll tweet something really daft and it will get nearly a million likes. I do like a bit of banter with my team-mates and to laugh at myself a bit too. It wasn't like I was saying, 'I'm going to show people I'm not boring.' If anything, people are probably even more likely to think I'm boring now, when I'm joking about trying to find the perfect Mini Egg or comparing biscuits with Robbo. But that's fine.

I believe you, Milly. Next question. Having seen you succumb to the temptation of going on social media, can we now expect you to change your mind on tattoos? If you were going to get tattooed, what would you get and what would be the meaning behind it?

I can see why people have tattoos of trophies they've won. But I have to say that, don't I, given what you've just had done on your thigh ... Jesús Navas had one on his hip of a goblin lifting the World Cup. It actually looked quite cool, so I could see why he did that, because it's a massive part of your life. But it's not really me, is it, Hendo? If I was going to do anything at all, it would be my kids' names or something like that. Or I could get a picture of you doing your fast feet before you lifted the European Cup. That would be good, wouldn't it?

But tattoos just aren't me. I would just worry about how it will look when I'm old and wrinkly. In about three years, before you say it.

You're a 'Sport Billy' who is annoyingly good at a lot of different sports, so if you could pick any other sportsperson to be, from the past or the present, who would it be?

Tiger Woods. No doubt at all. I started getting into golf when I was 15 or 16, which was when he was at his absolute peak. He was just spectacular to watch, with some of the shots he pulled off and the way he would drive the ball for miles at a time. The gap between first and second in the rankings was just ridiculous. To dominate a sport like he did, to make it so exciting to watch – and to widen the sport's appeal to a whole new audience – was just brilliant.

And then to go through everything he went through, with back surgery and a serious injury, and to come back to win the Tour Championship and then the Masters, when a lot of people thought he wouldn't even be able to swing a club again, was just amazing. A lot of people thought he was finished and wrote him off. I always said he would win a major again one day and I was buzzing when he did. I was watching the Masters with my mum, for some reason, and she was saying she rarely sees me get so excited about anything. But I was just buzzing that he had done it.

What he has done for the sport is incredible. When he plays, ticket sales and TV audiences go through the roof. Sales of golf clubs and golf equipment go through the roof. Participation the same. It's amazing what one person can do for a sport.

Ox did an appearance with him at a Nike event at Wembley. People say 'Don't meet your heroes – it's never the same,' but Ox said Tiger was great. He even let Ox use his putter for a putting challenge. If I met him, I would probably just irritate him by asking too many questions. Ox said he was just bombarding him with every question he could think of and Tiger didn't mind at all. He was a really nice guy, apparently. Cool as anything.

Match Day:
First Half

How important is it to make a strong start in a game? How do you go about that? James King

It's very important, both to set the right tempo on the pitch and to make sure the crowd are up for it. But a 'good start' can vary a lot, depending on what you're looking to get from a game. It depends what sort of tempo you want to set, which of course can change depending on the kind of team you're playing against.

You could go into an away game hoping to frustrate the opposition and the home crowd by stopping them building up a high tempo. We see that a lot when teams come to

Anfield. They'll be trying to slow things down and take their time from the very first minute, so it becomes a case of trying to force the tempo up and play the game on your terms rather than on their terms.

At Liverpool, like we did at City, we play on the front foot, looking to set our own tempo. But the way we do that can change, depending on the opposition. A lot of the time we'll try to press the opposition aggressively from the start, but some teams prefer just to sit deep and hit it long, so you put pressure on them in a different way. Sometimes, if it's less about building up a high tempo, we'll look to move the ball around more slowly at first. That can help the whole team settle into a game, with everyone getting plenty of touches early on.

If you're looking to make a strong, positive start, it's important to try to make something happen straight away. Obviously the best thing that can happen is that you score, but even if it's just creating a chance or winning a couple of early corners, giving the opposition something to think about, that can help to get the crowd going. If you're able to win the ball from the opposition once or twice in the early stages, even if nothing comes from it, that can help you set the right tempo and it makes everyone feel good. If it all starts a bit slowly and someone hits a pass into touch and the ball slips under someone's foot and out for a throw-in, that can have the opposite effect.

A classic example of the perfect start would be our game

at home to Huddersfield last season. We knew how they liked to play and we talked about trying to win the ball high up the pitch. We did just that and Naby scored after 15 seconds, but the flip-side of that is that we then had a bit of a lull. It was similar when we scored very early in the Champions League final. Obviously you would rather be 1–0 up than not, but sometimes it feels as if an early goal takes something out of you. I don't want to say it's a case of 'scoring too early' because you're always happy to score, but it does sometimes feel like it can have a negative effect on momentum. On a lot of other occasions we've been brilliant at scoring two or three goals in quick succession. It's not easy to explain. Every game is different.

Which is your favourite away ground?

Elland Road would be my favourite, obviously, but weirdly I've only played there once since I left in 2004 – and that was an England under-21 game. I've played against Leeds twice in cups (and the fans always chant 'You're Leeds and you know you are'), but never away. Playing at Camp Nou and the Bernabéu is special. I've got good memories of the Olympic Stadium in Rome – and the Wanda Metropolitano in Madrid is another one that I'll always remember now. Playing in the Maracanã for England against Brazil was a great experience. It was only a friendly, but it's one of those places where, even though it has been rebuilt, you can feel the history. Ox scored a brilliant goal there, actually. He doesn't like to mention that too often, as you can imagine.

Every player likes going to the grounds where they've done well in the past. I've always enjoyed going to Sunderland because I've scored a few goals there over the years – not just my first one for Leeds but an equaliser for Newcastle in a Tyne–Wear derby and a really nice one for Villa, where I caught it just right. I always get booed there because I played for Newcastle. But then again, I get booed at a lot of places. I get a few boos at Newcastle and Villa because I left them – not too many. I get booed at City because I left them. At Old Trafford they used to boo me as a Newcastle or Villa player just because I was ex-Leeds. As an ex-Leeds player who has played for City and now Liverpool, I tick just about every box there. We'll be playing at different grounds and the lads will say, 'Milly, why are you getting booed this time? What have you done to upset *this* lot?' 'Well . . .'

But I love playing at places like Old Trafford because it's always a big game. Even playing against them for Leeds under-10s and under-11s always felt huge. Getting booed doesn't bother me in the slightest. It drives me on, if anything. If I've been booed by Man United's fans for 15 years or more, I must be doing something right. As I said earlier, the only thing I don't like about Old Trafford is the away dressing room. They've made it smaller over the past couple of years, which is pretty backward when you consider that squad sizes and staff numbers have gone up and up. Fulham's is tiny too, but I don't think they've got enough room there, so that's a bit more understandable.

Best atmosphere you've ever played in? @aaronjacko

Some of the European nights at Anfield really stand out: Dortmund, City, Barcelona. But I've played in some really hostile atmospheres in away matches in the Champions League and Europa League over the years, too. Red Star Belgrade with Liverpool last season springs to mind, with all the flares going off and the incredible noise their fans were making. Another one was when I played for Newcastle away to Olympiacos in 2005. Rivaldo was playing for them, but what really made an impression on me that night was the atmosphere. They had two players sent off and their fans were going berserk. At one point I was racing to the touchline and I fell over one of the advertising hoardings and I thought it had started raining. But no, I was getting showered with spit. That's not nice, but it was a great experience to play in an atmosphere as hostile as that. I loved it.

Playing in Germany, there's always a fantastic atmosphere, like the Yellow Wall at Dortmund, but it's often in southern Europe where you really feel it most. Playing in Greece or Turkey is always an experience. Some of the Italian grounds too. The crowd are a long way from the pitch at

Napoli and Roma, but with the noise they make, you feel as if they're right on top of you.

When I talk about atmospheres like that, it's not just the noise they make in the ground. In some places, you feel the hostility almost from the moment you land at the airport the day before. I went to Napoli with City back in 2011 and their fans were singing and shouting outside our hotel all night. There were about 50 of them making a hell of a racket. When it got to 3am, they clocked off and another 50 took their place. It was all so well organised. We're used to getting police escorts to the stadium, but in Naples there were fans on mopeds chasing the police escort, driving alongside us and weaving in and out of the traffic and onto the pavement so they could throw stuff at our bus. Even when we went for a little stroll on the morning of the game, we were getting chased. It hasn't been quite that hostile when I've been back there since, which makes me think their issue that time was with Roberto Mancini.

Coming to Anfield with other teams, I always found it hostile. I liked playing in atmospheres like that, but I think I only ever won one game here before I joined Liverpool. That was with Villa. It's safe to say I prefer it with the home crowd on my side.

Do the fans genuinely play a part in the result of a game?
@hazpjhazpj

They certainly do at times, but I'm probably the wrong person to ask because I've never really been able to get my head around the whole home-or-away thing. That will probably sound like a bit of a contradiction when I've raved about how inspiring the atmosphere has been on some of those big European nights we've had at Liverpool, but atmospheres like that aren't the norm, not even at Anfield.

Clearly there are times when an atmosphere really inspires a team, or intimidates the away team, but I've never really gone for the whole notion of home advantage. You want to believe it when you're playing a home game, but half the games we play are away. Do I think the home team have got an advantage over us in those games? Only if you allow yourself to think they have.

You would always rather have a hostile crowd on your side than on your opponents' side, but ultimately it's 11 against 11 on a football pitch and, unless you have the wrong mentality, it shouldn't affect you. When I was at City, we had a great team but we always had a poor record at Anfield – but I couldn't say, hand on heart, that it was because of the atmosphere. I always looked forward to coming here as a visiting player. I think you relish atmospheres like that. You should do anyway.

Not every player does, though. I've seen a number of

players over the years who don't play anything like as well away from home. For whatever reason, they don't seem to travel well. They would probably understand the home/away thing more than I do.

How much do you notice the crowd when you're playing? How much does it make a difference?

You're always aware of it. You try to have tunnel vision and block out everything else, but you're not in a bubble. Sometimes you're inspired by it. I'll keep mentioning our Champions League games at Anfield against City and Barcelona and the Europa League game against Dortmund a few years back. Against Barcelona we had a corner in the second minute and the roar that went up was just amazing – not for a goal, for a corner. It's quite rare that something like that really makes an impression on me during a game. Another was when I was playing for City against Man United in the FA Cup semi-final at Wembley, where the entire City end started doing the 'Poznan' and dancing around. It felt like the whole of Wembley was shaking. I would say it's certain games, rather than something you're always aware of.

A great atmosphere can inspire a team, but the opposite can happen too. Sometimes you're playing in an atmosphere where the home crowd are on their team's back. I've been on both ends of that. There were times at Newcastle when the fans were raging at the team – and justifiably so. They pay their money and, if the team aren't performing, they have a right to say what they want. Does it help players if you get on their back? Some might say it spurs them on, but most would probably say the opposite. If the home crowd are on their team's back, that's generally good news for the away team. I've played in atmospheres like that where we've been 4–0 or 5–0 up away from home and the home team have been getting pelters from their crowd. You almost feel sorry for them.

It can be difficult to perform in that kind of atmosphere. Some players go into their shell. In that situation, you've just got to get your head down, try to get on the ball and build something, or just try to make a tackle or do anything that will change the mood – both on the pitch and in the stands. The last thing any player wants is to be accused of 'hiding' – not wanting the ball, not wanting to take responsibility or put your head above the parapet. It's not nice, but you've just got to keep going and do the best for your team.

Does the weather ever bother you? Are there any conditions you hate playing in? James King

The worst is when it's really hot and humid, which usually means pre-season abroad. I'll take the cold any day – even if it's minus 15 degrees in Russia – and rain doesn't bother me either. But when it's roasting, like in South Bend, Indiana, in pre-season, you're desperate for it to cool down. And you can't even put sun cream on your face because it gets in your eyes.

Playing in the wind isn't great either. I'm not doing the whole 'Could he do it on a windy night at Stoke?' thing, but it always seems to be blowing a gale there. Two corners of the ground are exposed and the wind whips around inside, so it can be difficult to play. It was always a tough away trip anyway, even without having to battle against the elements as they were hurling throw-ins towards your six-yard box.

What is the funniest thing you've ever heard from the crowd?

I'm sure there's a lot I don't hear because I'm so focused on the game. Unless it's totally quiet, which is rare, the only time you really hear them is when you're warming up or when you're on the touchline. I remember getting pelters from West Ham's fans at Upton Park one year when I was warming up – and then their players started warming up and they got even worse, which took the pressure right off us. I'll give you a few of my favourites from down the years.

1) In the early days at Leeds, when I was warming up as substitute, there would be a lot of 'Oi, Milner, does your mum know you're out?' Or 'Milner, you spotty little bastard.' Or just 'Pizza face.' When I was playing an FA Cup tie at Scunthorpe on my 17th birthday, there was

one guy shouting, 'See you tonight in the Old Ball for a birthday drink,' which was the pub at the end of my parents' street. That was a bit odd.

2) One that really made me laugh was at Stoke a few years ago when I was at City. I was playing on the wing and David Silva was bringing the ball towards me, so I made a run, and then David played a pass to someone else – and this bloke shouted out, 'Oi, Milner – you're just a f***ing decoy!' I never expected to hear 'decoy' as an insult, but, yes, the guy was pretty perceptive. I was genuinely laughing at that one.

3) And one thing I've heard quite a few times is 'Milner, you fat b*****d.' The first time one of the other lads heard that, he was like, 'Fat? Wow.' There are a lot of things I will take before the word 'b*****d' – ugly, spotty, thick, Yorkshire, boring – but I never thought 'fat' was one I would get. I was almost tempted to whip my top off. Almost.

Who has been your most difficult opponent?

I've played against all the great players of my generation – Lionel Messi, Cristiano Ronaldo, Xavi, Andrés Iniesta and so on. The best player, in my opinion, is Messi. Let's be honest, you've probably seen the nutmeg on YouTube ... But I would honestly say the one who has troubled me most on a one-to-one basis is Wilfried Zaha. I've been sent off twice for Liverpool and they've both been for fouls against him. He's such a difficult opponent, not just because he's got great ability but because he's so unpredictable. With most players, if you're up against them, one to one, you've got a good idea what they're going to do. Zaha is a nightmare to play against.

What is the relationship on the pitch with the opposition? Do you talk with them? If so, what? Is it hostile? @FootieTiger

There isn't much dialogue. If you've got a mate on the opposition team, it's normally just a quick hello before-hand – either in the tunnel or in the warm-up – and then I've got my game face on. I just get on with it. I'll chat to them afterwards. If there's a break in play, you might make a throwaway comment, but it's not likely to be 'How's the missus? How are the kids getting on?' It would be weird to have an actual conversation with someone during a game.

Most players are the same – totally focused while the game is going on. And then occasionally you get someone like Jimmy Bullard, who was just . . . mad. I remember when I was at Villa we had a game at Hull and he was 'on one' from the moment the game kicked off. He was just non-stop. We were running down the wing, trying to get ahead of each other, and he just said something ridiculous to make me laugh. It's probably the only time I've ever been laughing out loud during a Premier League game. The stretcher-bearers came on and he was messing about with them. I'd never known anything like it. He was hilarious, really good fun.

It can be funny when you're in direct opposition with a good mate. I came up against Stephen Warnock in an FA Cup tie for City against Leeds at the Etihad. I was right wing and he was left-back. We both love a tackle and we seemed to spend the whole game kicking lumps out of each other. He hit me with one early on, then I got him back. Then he hit me with an even harder one, then I did the same. It just escalated like that the whole game. They weren't nasty or cynical challenges, but they were hard – very hard – fair tackles. God knows what someone like David Silva made of it. Warny and I had a good laugh about it afterwards. Just to be clear, though, Warny started it.

Back when I first started, you used to get a fair bit of trash talk on the pitch. I remember as a young lad, opponents would try to intimidate me. I would hear people shouting to their team-mates, 'Snap him' or 'Break his legs'. That doesn't happen now, but it was par for the course at that time. Most of the time they were just trying to shake you up, so you would have to try to ignore it, but there was a lot more leeway to make bad challenges. People used to say the first tackle was free in those days: that is, you could catch someone late and you wouldn't even get booked. A few opposition full-backs used to take advantage of that when they were up against a little teenage winger.

I would never have imagined in those days that I would be sent off in my career. Back then, you had to do a really bad tackle to get sent off. But I've been sent off twice at Liverpool for second bookable offences, which on both occasions were the type of tackles that wouldn't even have got a booking back then. There's a lot more protection for players and a lot less leeway if you get your timing wrong.

There's also a lot less naughty stuff now. You used to get opponents trampling all over your toes or nipping you on the waist at corners or picking you up by the armpit hair when they'd fouled you. You don't tend to get any of that now. There are so many cameras, you wouldn't get away with it.

How do you interact with a team-mate during the game when they aren't playing well? Do you offer advice or just boost confidence? @addonnn

It depends really. You've got to look at the situation, consider the team-mate's personality and try to get a sense of what he'll react best to. You can either give him an arm around the shoulder, or you can give him a rocket. I prefer the arm around the shoulder or a bit of an encouragement. If a player has made a bad mistake or he's having a really poor game or he's feeling nervous, I'll usually try to say, 'Just forget about it. It's gone. Let it go.' Especially with a young player, you have to let them know that it's not a

Left. Playing for England under-17s against Brazil in July 2002, unaware how close I was getting to the big time.

Right. 'Did you have a bet on 4–4 or what?' Making my Premier League debut for Leeds away to West Ham as a 16-year-old in November 2002.

Above. Somewhere underneath Jonathan Woodgate, Gary Kelly and Alan Smith is a 16-year-old whose dream has just come true, scoring the winner against Chelsea at Elland Road in 2002.

Right. Saluting the crowd after that goal against Chelsea a week before my 17th birthday. One of the proudest moments of my career.

'Right, where's the new lad? Where is he?' All smiles after signing for Newcastle United, along with Nicky Butt, but my time under Sir Bobby Robson was too brief.

There aren't many better feelings than scoring a goal, particularly against Manchester United when you've been walloped by Gary Neville a few minutes earlier.

The celebration? It's a long story involving my mate Smudge, the Villa masseur. Delighted after putting Villa 1–0 up against Manchester United in the League Cup final, but the day ended in frustration.

Eagerly looking forward to a press conference on England duty. Like a nightwatchman in cricket, I always seemed to be sent out when they needed someone to face the awkward deliveries with a straight bat.

Being substituted is a horrible feeling. When it's half an hour into your first ever appearance at a World Cup, it's even worse – even if you know you weren't fit to play in the first place.

The final years of my England career were frustrating, but wearing the captain's armband against Holland at Wembley in March 2016 was an honour.

Above, left. FA Cup final day, 2011, thrilled to get my hands on Manchester City's first trophy in 35 years.

Above, right. 'Why always you?' Mario Balotelli could test your patience as a team-mate – particularly if he parked near you at the training ground – but, when he was in the mood, he was a match-winner for City.

Below. 'Aguerooooooooooo!' Celebrating the most incredible end to the 2011–12 season as Manchester City win the Premier League title in stoppage time.

Liverpool v Manchester City, 2016. When you're stuck between not wanting to celebrate against your old club and wanting to keep a promise to your new team-mates . . .

Offering Lionel Messi a pick-me-up during the Champions League semi-final first leg in 2019. I don't think he took it. Fair enough.

Above. Kiev 2018. Walking past the biggest prize in European football, knowing I can't touch it, not even wanting to look at it, wondering if I'll ever get that close to it again . . .

Right. Oh, what a difference a year makes. In fact, Champions League glory tasted even sweeter after all the pain we'd suffered over the previous few years.

Above. The scenes on the victory parade through Liverpool city centre the next day. Incredible.

Left. Here we go again. Pre-season training at the University of Notre Dame, Indiana, in 2019.

matter of life and death. I would urge him to get on the ball, get a good feel of it, play his way back into the game with a few easy passes and start again.

There are other things you can do. If they're having a difficult time defensively, you can try to help them with that. I'm in a position where, if one of the full-backs is struggling, I can give a bit of support and help during a difficult spell so that he's not left one on one. If he's having a difficult time on the ball, I can drop deep to receive a pass from him and give it back again just so he gets a few easy passes under his belt and starts to feel more comfortable in possession. One of the great things about being in a team is that, in that kind of situation, everyone can pull together to help a player through it.

It's not just about what you do on the pitch. You can try to set the right mood around the dressing room, on the bus to the game, in the hotel and so on. There's a fine line between too little pressure and too much. There's such a thing as being too relaxed, but you don't want the mood to be so intense and so nervous that a player goes onto the pitch terrified and feeling like the world is falling apart if he makes a mistake. If a player spends all day cooped up in a hotel thinking, 'Huge game tonight. Imagine if I mess up,' then that's going to cause problems. Especially with young players, you need to try to help them feel relaxed – determined and focused, but relaxed. It's about getting the balance right.

What about when you're the one struggling? If you've mis-placed a few passes, how do you stop things spiralling?

It happens sometimes. Everyone has bad days at the office. Every player has days when things don't go well. There are two ways you can react to that. Do you hide and try to escape unscathed until the end of the game or until you get subbed? Or do you try to do something about it and turn a negative into a positive?

I don't think I've ever been one for hiding, but there were probably times earlier in my career when I worried about the next pass or thought, 'I'm not going to try that pass now, because of how the last one went.' But you can't afford to be like that. If you give the ball away three times running, forget it, it's gone, move on. If you asked me what my worst ever performance was, or my worst ever mistake, I would struggle to pick anything out because I've tried to wipe it from my mind. The older I've got, the better I've become at moving on from mistakes, rather than worrying.

It depends what sort of position you play and how the game is going. If you're playing wide and you're not seeing much of the ball, yes you can go looking for it, but you don't want to leave your full-back exposed. You need to have the discipline to hold your position and keep the team's shape, even if you're struggling. It must be harder in that those circumstances for a centre-forward or a big target man who thrives on service, like Andy Carroll. Yes, you can compete when the ball is pumped forward, but a lot of the time you just have to stay patient and ready for the opportunities when they come.

There's more opportunity to be involved as a midfielder. You might be having an absolute shocker on the ball, where you feel like you couldn't pass water, but you just have to try to get on the ball, make a few passes and play your way back into the game. And if you can't do that, well, at least you can run around and make a nuisance of yourself and do well on that side of the game. Games can be won without the ball as well as with it. If that's the worst you can do in a game – defending well, tracking back, running off the ball, doing a job for the team – then it's still a lot better than hiding.

At Home . . .

Being a footballer in the football-crazy cities that you have been, how is it? Are you able to walk the streets or go shopping etc.? @Chris_Cadaret

I don't spend that much time in the city centres, but the impression I get is that Liverpool is a bit more hectic than Manchester in that respect. Newcastle was like that too. Leeds, Newcastle, Birmingham, Manchester, Liverpool, they're all great football cities. I've always lived outside the city, wherever I've played, because I think it's good to be able to get away from the buzz, but of course you do spend some time in the centres. Yes, you get stopped and yes, you can feel people staring at you, which is something I do find a bit uncomfortable, but 99 per cent of people are very friendly and respectful. So yes, you can walk the streets.

Do you get annoyed with people asking for photos? Alfie Thompson

No. It's nice that there are people who want a photo or an autograph. There will be the odd occasion where you're out for a meal and someone will come up to you when you're eating, mid-slurp on your spaghetti, or one of the kids has just thrown up, and they'll still ask and at moments like that you think, 'I'm just a bit busy here, mate . . .' In that situation I might ask someone to come back when I've finished eating, but I'll still find a way to do it. There might be days where you've lost and you're in a foul mood and you think you could do without it, but as footballers we know we're in a very privileged position where we can make someone's day by giving them just a few seconds of our time.

One thing that is annoying is when people don't ask and they just take a picture of you – a sly one – or they're filming you without your permission. That is a bit out of order, isn't it? Sometimes they think they're doing it discreetly and then the flash goes off and they put it down, pretending they weren't doing it. I know people will say, 'You're in the limelight, you get paid that much money,' and yeah, that's true. I just prefer it if people ask.

The one time I can remember refusing a photo is when

a guy shouted abuse at me and then asked for a picture afterwards. That's the wrong way round, isn't it? Usually, if someone's a Man United fan or whatever, they'll tell me after they've got their picture – as if they think I would refuse if they told me first. But that guy I mentioned abused me first and then asked for a picture. Sorry, but no. That's not how it works. But that's one person. The vast majority are great. The people who ask are no trouble at all.

If you're in the supermarket, do you ever look at the price of anything? @stephenspierin

I'm from Yorkshire, so of course I do. And sometimes I screw my face up and put the item down again. I'm sure there are times when I don't look at the price – if I need kidney beans or whatever – but other times I'll look and think, 'How much?! Well I'm not having that.' If this is the old politician's question about whether footballers know how much a pint of milk is, then yes I do, which is why I'd rather buy a two-litre bottle instead. Bargain.

Amy loves a bargain when she's food shopping. She'll come back with three packs of something. 'It was three for £5.' 'Yeah, but you've saved 20p and we don't need the third one . . . or the second one, for that matter.'

There's this image of the 'flash footballer', but I don't think many of us are. I don't think you can call someone 'flash' just because they've got a nice car or a nice house.

You get some footballers who are the other extreme. Teddy Lučić, a great lad, turned up at Leeds in a battered old Volvo and wouldn't even think of changing it. Alan Smith had a phone that was 15 years old and a car that was knackered. He would open his boot to get his golf clubs and all this junk would fall out – not just old kit but England caps and all sorts.

I know people have this image of footballers and their wives throwing money around like confetti, but I can't think of many players I've met in my career who have really lived up to that stereotype. I know it might look that way when you read about a player paying $1,000 in a restaurant for a gold-plated steak, but that isn't the norm. It made headlines because it's *not* the norm. But it's this kind of stuff that sticks in people's minds – it has stuck in my mind, to be honest – so that ends up shaping their opinions of footballers. If we're doing things for charities and doing community work, which every footballer does to some degree, it's not going to get the same exposure. Negative stories always get so much more exposure than positive stories.

There's nothing wrong with people having nice things. As long as you're trying to help out in other ways – public appearances and community work and foundations and charities – you shouldn't feel guilty about buying a nice car. If you like cars and you get paid good money, why wouldn't you buy a nice car? Everyone has the right to treat themselves if they're able to. There's nothing wrong with that as long as you're using your position to try to give something back in other ways. I can see how it invites criticism if you're being flash by posting stuff all over Instagram, showing off your possessions, but again, that isn't the norm.

Most players on good money will have a nice car and a nice house, but that's no different from any other walk of life. Most players will also invest their money sensibly and they'll help out charities and things like that. That's normal. It's what you would expect. It's their money and they're entitled to do what they want with it, but I really don't think the majority of footballers are the way we're portrayed.

Is there anything that you would love to do, but aren't allowed to do as a footballer? Esme Kay

I've never been on a jet-ski. That looks pretty good fun, but it's one of those things we're not allowed to do as footballers. It doesn't specifically mention jet-skis in con-tracts – not in mine, anyway – but it does say something about not indulging in any dangerous activity or anything that might put your fitness and availability at risk, so it's clearly off-limits. Likewise skiing, paragliding and anything like that. I quite like the idea of jumping out of a plane. It would terrify me because I'm not great with heights, but I do think it would be an incredible experience. Maybe I'll try that when I've retired – if I'm feeling brave enough to do it.

Skiing looks good fun. I had one team-mate who wasn't

really playing and was being phased out by the manager, being told to play with the kids, and he just didn't care any more. He took up snowboarding, while he was still under contract, and spent so much time doing it that he got amazing at it. He was doing jumps and all sorts.

I've heard a few players say the first thing they want to do when they retire is to buy a motorbike. That wouldn't interest me at all. They're death traps.

How do you deal with 24/7 social media and keeping your family life out of the spotlight? @cj7toon

I tend not to put anything family-related on social media. Everyone is different, but my view has always been that my private life should be precisely that: private. There are some parts of your life that are just for you and your family. You need a certain amount of time and space to yourselves. I don't think it should be open house for everything.

I think there's an unnecessary burden on players' wives. Maybe some wives and girlfriends are comfortable with that spotlight, but Amy has never been interested in that side of it. We've been together since we were teenagers. She wants to be with me for me, not because I'm a footballer or because I'm 'famous'. People talk about that 'WAG' lifestyle, but it's not all glamour. There's a lot of time Amy is on her own or she's having to deal with all the mood swings a footballer goes through – the ups, the downs, injuries – and all the strange routines, like eating and sleeping at weird times, and irregular hours and me going to a hotel the night before a game and so on. She's been living with that for 18 years.

The children know that their dad is a footballer, but they're only now beginning to see that it's not the norm and that there are certain things that come with that. Amy and I just want them to have a normal childhood and enjoy themselves. It's going to be up to them how they live their lives, but we wouldn't want to force anything on them. If we were to put them in the spotlight, I think that invites a certain pressure straight away.

When I walk into school and drop the kids off, I sometimes get greeted with 'Hi Milner' or 'You lost the other day' and, at their age, I really don't want their relationships with other kids defined by having my surname. I know it's inevitable that it will crop up in conversations, but it could get nasty as they get older. You do hear of that. I will probably have retired before they're at the age where it could get really nasty, but kids can be cruel – especially if they're repeating something they've heard their parents say. It's hard enough growing up anyway. That would make it worse.

The flip-side of all of this is that my boy loves going on the pitch after the game. He did after the last Premier League game of last season, against Wolves, and loved it. Then he came to the Champions League final and our families ended up joining us on the pitch for the celebrations and pictures and so on. He loved that too. So obviously that's a perk. But as a rule, we like to keep family life as private as possible. Other people might have a different view, which is perfectly fine, but we feel keeping a low profile is the right thing for us.

Which app do you use most?

WhatsApp is the one that's buzzing constantly, with various groups. One app that I love – it's not exactly a new one – is Shazam, where any time you hear a song you like, you can find out what it is and download it straight away.

In terms of apps I use for my profession, I use Runkeeper when I'm doing a run. Another really good one is Intervals. If we're given a session where it's, say, four-minute sessions of 45 seconds of hard running followed by 15 seconds resting, or something like that, you can customise all of that with Intervals. You can have your music on and it still counts you in and out. It's another of those where I can't remember how I lived without it.

How much football do most players watch?

In my case, less than I used to. When I was younger, I would watch everything. These days, I'm away such a lot of the time and then when I'm at home with a free afternoon, it's more likely to be Nickelodeon than Sky Sports on in our house. Certain games I'll watch, but when we were going for the Premier League title last season, neck and neck with City, I went out of my way *not* to watch their games. I couldn't affect the outcome, so why waste energy getting worked up and stressed by watching them? They're a great team to watch, but I found it was beneficial to me to turn the TV off, put the phone away and catch up afterwards.

There are players who hardly watch any football. There are others who will go home and watch every single game they can. A lot of managers are obsessive and can't believe it if you haven't watched a certain game the night before. I watch plenty, but in terms of watching future opponents, we get a really good briefing about the opposition before we play them, so it isn't as important from a homework perspective as it used to be.

What's it like to be a footballer watching a match in the stadium as a fan? @AndrewHaigh

If you're talking about watching my own team, I find it unbearable. I can't stand it. I think most players would say the same. We're a brilliant team to watch, but if I'm injured or suspended and I'm watching from the stand, I find it really difficult. I want to be out there, helping my team. When I'm not involved, the frustration levels are massive. I don't feel like I can enjoy it at all, which I know sounds ridiculous when I'm talking about a team as good as ours.

If you're talking about watching Leeds, it's not something

I've done very often since they sold me when I was 18. I went to watch them in the play-off final against Watford – the less said about that, the better. You can't really do the whole 'fan' thing when you're playing for another club, but I always follow Leeds' results avidly – the same as Robbo does with Celtic, for example. I'll always watch Leeds games on TV. For the play-offs earlier this year, I was down in Woburn, playing golf, and the hotel where we were didn't have Sky, so we were struggling to find anywhere that was showing it and then we found this tiny pub with ceilings so low that people had to stoop down to stand at the bar. It was such a random place to watch a massive game like that, but I ended up watching it in there with my uncle, who's a Leeds fan, and his mate. It was all going so well and then the keeper unfortunately made a mistake and the game was gone.

¿Qué es lo más difícil de aprender castellano? ¿Cuáles son los trucos que has usado para aprender? @redfan4ver

Creo que cuando aprendes otro idioma, siempre es difícil. Es más sencillo al principio. 'Me llamo James Milner, vivo en Inglaterra.' En castellano las conjugaciones de los verbos son difíciles. Eso es lo más difícil para mí. Mi mujer Amy aprende también conmigo y cuando empezamos con los verbos, fueron muy difíciles para ella. Lo más imprescindible desde mi punto de vista, cuando aprendes una lengua, es no tener miedo cuando hablas. Si dices algo incorrecto, no hay problema. Si tienes amigos españoles, es importante practicar con ellos. Si alguien está aprendiendo y comete un error, no te rías de él.

Intento hablar con mis niños en castellano. No siempre hacen las cosas bien, pero la mente de los niños es increíble, es como una esponja. Mis niños niños entienden bastante. No hablan tanto, pero repiten algunas cosas, algunas palabras. Pero sobre todo entienden los imperativos: 'siéntate', 'ven aquí', 'ten cuidado' . . . Las cosas que un padre les dice a sus niños.

Why do you speak to your children in Spanish?

The idea initially came from Gaël Clichy. His wife spoke to their daughter in English, so he decided he would speak to her in French, so that they could learn both languages. Their nanny or cleaner spoke another language, so their daughter understood all three. That made an impression on me because I was already learning Spanish, so I felt that, if I could speak to my two in Spanish, that would give them a base in a second language. If they then end up having proper lessons with a teacher in school, they should be able to pick it up quite easily. Then, once they've got that base, they should be able to learn French or another language quite easily too and then, without even having to try that hard, they might have two or three languages under their belt by the time they leave school.

I've always been impressed when I've heard players from other countries switching easily from one language to another. I was buying a place in Spain a few years ago, so I thought 'Why not learn the language?' I would probably have found it easier to learn Spanish when I was at school than it is to learn it as an adult. I'm not fluent – you would have to live somewhere to be fluent – and there's plenty I don't know, but whatever I need to say, I can find a way to say it. I'm sure I miss the odd word, and there are better ways of saying certain things, but I can have a conversation comfortably now.

In fact, I got sucked into doing an interview in Spanish on the pitch after the Champions League final. I thought it was going to be in English, but the reporter just started asking me in Spanish, so I had to answer in Spanish. I haven't seen it back, but I think I got away with it.

Outside of football, who is the most famous person whose number is on your phone? Do you have any 'showbiz' friends?

'Showbiz' isn't really my scene. It's mostly footballers or other friends I've made through football or my mates from home. Your friends change as you get older, but I've still got friends from school, and we'll get together a few times a year. Either they'll come to matches and I'll see them there or I'll give them a call when I'm back home in Leeds and we'll go and play snooker together or something.

But I've got to know Gary Barlow, who very kindly performed at my foundation's annual ball. He's a Liverpool fan, which helps. Likewise Olly Murs – but he supports Manchester United, so I'm not sure I can really call him a friend, can I? Any 'showbiz' connections I've made have tended to be through the foundation. Another one is Simon Rix, the bass player from Kaiser Chiefs. He's a big Leeds fan. We message each other quite a lot.

Usually, though, the friends I make are through sport, like Jimmy Anderson, who is a patron of my foundation. There are a few golfers that I've become good friends with. I get on well with Tyrrell Hatton. I got to know him through his caddy at the time. Tyrrell is a funny guy. You see him on the course and he's explosive, in a way that is quite unusual in golf, and he sometimes gets criticised for losing his head and so on, but when you meet him, he's the complete opposite of what you might imagine. He's got a great sense of humour and he'll joke about how he shouldn't have reacted like that. He's just desperate to win and he wears his heart on his sleeve.

What do you do with your medals?

I've heard of some people saying they keep their medals in their sock drawer or they can't even remember where they are. They're in a trophy cabinet at home along with a few other special items, man-of-the-match awards and things like that. I've got a shirt from every team I've played for, including my first England shirt, which has been signed by everyone who played in that game. When I won my 50th England cap, I was presented with a photo montage thing which, again, had been signed by my team-mates. That was nice. I was given a special award when I made my 500th Premier League appearance last year. There's space for me to add a few more medals before I retire.

. . . And Away

What are pre-season tours like? A great way to see the world? Or is it just constant travelling without actually getting to see anything? Ben Smith

I wouldn't say they're a great way to see the world, because the reality is that wherever we go, we're there to train and to play matches. There isn't much downtime and we're never anywhere for long, so it's not as if we're able to do much sightseeing.

This year, as well as games against Tranmere and Bradford, we had matches in South Bend, Boston, New York, Edinburgh and Geneva. Last year we went to Charlotte, New York and Michigan. And if you're a footballer on a preseason tour, that doesn't really mean visiting different cities.

It just means different hotels, different training pitches, different stadiums. That's a pretty sad way of putting it, but it's basically true.

The matches themselves can be challenging in ways you wouldn't expect. Sometimes the pitches aren't the best. Or if we're in America, we're sometimes playing on baseball pitches, which is a bit weird in itself. If you're playing in America in July, it's roasting hot. In parts of Asia, it's very humid or it's monsoon weather. I remember going to Thailand and Hong Kong in my first pre-season with Newcastle and I'd never seen rain like it. It was winter in Australia when we went there. We had one game where it was Baltic. Some of the lads had rugs on the bench.

You don't get much chance to look around. Someone said to me, 'How was New York? It looked like you had a bit of time to explore.' I think that was just because I put one picture from Central Park on Instagram. We went for a pre-match walk – in tracksuits, sweating like pigs, with a line of security around us. We were out for about 25 minutes and then went back to the hotel. We actually had a few hours free the night before the game, so we walked down Fifth Avenue, had a bit of a look around and went for a coffee. It wasn't long enough to do any proper sightseeing and it's not as if you could go out to a bar or go for a meal or watch a show or anything like that. In Boston we went to Fenway Park and to the club shop and then we did a community event. Other than that, it was training and playing matches.

That's the thing about pre-season. Training-wise, it's the most intense period of the season. You're training two or sometimes three times a day and you're also doing a lot of commercial and community activities, because there are always those elements to a tour as well. The staff will sometimes manage a night out and a chance to get more of a feel for a place, but for the rest of us, it's more like a scouting trip – just having a very quick look at somewhere and trying to get a sense of whether it would be worth coming back with the family.

We've been to Hong Kong, Bangkok and Kuala Lumpur since I've been at Liverpool, but I can hardly say I've 'done' those places. They all look amazing and the people are so incredibly friendly, but we just don't really get the chance to do anything. And often it's monsoon season or it's incredibly humid – and either way, the pitches can be difficult. And you're in pre-season anyway, so you're training extremely hard and you're exhausted in the evenings and . . . you probably get the picture. It's not the ideal way to see the world. I need to travel in Asia properly when I retire – go back to those places, go to China and Japan and so on. It's somewhere I would love to take the family when the children are old enough to appreciate what it's about.

One thing that always sticks with me, though, is the people. The supporters are totally fanatical and you feel like you'll get mobbed if you go anywhere. The turnout we get is amazing. So when we had a couple of hours' free time in Hong Kong, a few of us just went into Starbucks around the corner from our hotel because it was pretty much empty. By the time we ordered our drinks, word had clearly got around and there were about 50 fans waiting outside. A couple of minutes later there were twice as many of them again. And – I'm sure you wouldn't get this in many other parts of the world – they just formed an orderly queue around the mall. So we took turns, where one of us would go down the line, signing things, posing for pictures and so on, so that the rest of the lads could enjoy their coffee. It was a pretty good system really, but we started to realise that once their things had been signed, they were running around the back to get to the end of the line so they could get another picture or whatever. It was pretty clever. You had to admire it. But they were so polite.

Then there was Hendo's biggest fan. One year we went to Thailand, Australia and Malaysia in pre-season. We got off the plane at Bangkok and there was this woman waiting in arrivals with this big flashing 'Jordan Henderson' sign. We got to Brisbane for the next leg of the trip a few days later and she was there again. We got to Kuala Lumpur – same again! Everywhere we went, she was always there waiting for us with her flashing sign. I don't know how she did it, but three different countries and she beat us there every time.

But back to your question, pre-season is a slog. It doesn't tend to be fun – and that just makes it more frustrating when you're somewhere that you would love to look around. I had it with a few of the lads this summer, when I had a holiday in Chicago, which is a fantastic city. They were saying, 'Oh, yeah, Chicago. We went for pre-season, didn't we? Everyone says it's great.' Until you go somewhere properly – not in pre-season – you don't really have a clue what the place is like.

In 2017 we had an end-of-season tour of Australia. Sorry, did I say tour? What I mean is, we had a flying visit to Sydney. We had the final game of the season against Middlesbrough at Anfield on the Sunday afternoon and then set off for Sydney on the Monday evening, flying through the night, stopping in Phuket to refuel. Some of the staff and the ex-players who had travelled with us were doing a fair bit of 'refuelling' of their own on the flight. The phrase 'flying pub' was used and it's fair to say they were in high spirits by the time we got to Phuket. Not so Joe Gomez, who had somehow got mumps. Poor Joe had to stay the night at the airport in Phuket and fly straight home again. The rest of us carried on to Sydney and I think by the time we arrived, with the time difference, it was Wednesday morning – and we were playing the match that evening.

I couldn't play because I had picked up a stiff back, so that wasn't great. We had Steven Gerrard, Jamie Carragher, Steve McManaman and Daniel Agger in the squad and they all played well, actually. Under the circumstances, everyone did well to perform. Then we went to bed and got up the next morning to do some promotional appearances. We were all exhausted, but it was great fun. The manager went for an Australian cultural experience, where the locals had him trying to play the didgeridoo and throw a boomerang. Gini, Dej and others went to a children's hospital. Trent, Bobby and Lucas went to Bondi Beach to try a bit of surfing. I was in a group with Ads and Studge and we took a boat across Sydney Harbour to the zoo. Studge was given a GoPro camera to take round the zoo and the plan was run the video on the club website, but he seemed to get a bit distracted by what the koalas were doing to each other, so it never saw the light of day.

After that, it was time to fly home. But not for me. I flew on to America for my holiday and met up with the family in Florida. I didn't have a clue what day it was when I got there.

Do you read a book on the coach or plane when travelling?
@davepperlmutter

I used to read a lot, especially on holiday, but less so these days. I'll listen to audiobooks when I'm driving to training, rather than always having music or the radio on. A lot of sports autobiographies, which won't surprise you. I enjoyed Graeme Souness's. Peter Crouch's was great, particularly because he reads it himself – very funny guy, Crouchy. It's quite varied what I listen to. I've just listened to one about a guy who had a Navy SEAL come and live with him. I've also been listening to a Spanish one to help me with the language.

What do players do to avoid boredom when away on tours or at tournaments? Joe McGuinness

If I think back to when I first started going away with England under-21s, I would take a big portable DVD player with me and a load of DVDs. I remember being into *24* and I would take the entire box set away with me. It seemed like everyone was into it, but we would all be up to different stages in it, all sitting with these massive DVD players on the bus. Occasionally you would catch a glimpse of someone else's screen and see a spoiler. 'Oh, so she's on the other side? I wish I hadn't just seen that . . .'

It's so much easier these days with iPads and everyone's got Sky or Netflix. I've got films, TV programmes and games on there. Robbo says I'm like the App Store's dream customer because I'm always downloading games. I like ones that have a bit of strategy to them. There's one I've been into recently which is puzzle-based and, from completing these various puzzles, you have to build a city. It's pretty pointless really, but if it keeps your mind ticking over and stops you getting bored, it serves a purpose.

I've played *FIFA* a fair bit in my time. Joleon Lescott was the main man for that. I played *Call of Duty* a bit when I was younger. I've never played *Fortnite*, which a lot of the younger players are into. TV-wise I like a good drama. In pre-season this year I got into *La Casa de Papel*, which in the UK is called *Money Heist*. It's a Spanish story, but it's dubbed in English or you can use subtitles. It's about a group of people who are custom-picked to rob a bank. It's a good watch anyway, but I also like it because it helps with my Spanish. I've been watching *Take Us Home*, the fly-on-the-wall documentary about last season at Leeds. That's really good.

Some of us play cards when we're on the bus or flying somewhere. It's all very controlled these days. I've been on buses in the past where there has been heavy gambling and lads have lost massive sums of money. That can't be good, going onto the pitch with that hanging over you, can it? I don't really think that happens now. We play cards a lot at Liverpool, some of us, but generally we're playing trumps or hearts and it's only for bragging rights – or if it is for money, it's only very small stakes. You always have to be careful with Robbo because if he loses, he'll give you his Scottish currency. I know it's legal tender, but you try telling that to some of the shops near where I live. Cheers, Robbo.

Sometimes a load of us get into a certain game. In the build-up to the Champions League final in Kiev, it was *Stick Golf*. That got quite competitive. The next season we moved on to *Tenable*, the TV quiz show. We would all do it together, taking turns to give answers. Inevitably, there were punishments for those who got a question wrong. If you were lucky, you would get away with a flick on the ear.

And where it gets really competitive is when we're playing actual sports, rather than cards or games or quiz shows. We were away for three weeks in pre-season, so there was a lot of table tennis being played. Virgil is very good. So is Joe Gomez. Dej and Mo were always playing against each other – and Dej would be complaining that Mo was too defensive and just patted it straight back every time. Mo and Hendo ended up winning, but you know what it's like with a big group of lads. Everyone thinks they're the best. No one can ever accept defeat in those matches. I certainly can't.

When we were away with England, we used to play that table-tennis game where you knock the ball back and then you run around the table and everyone is constantly on the move. Because there were only two bats, we had to improvise. If there were any PlayStation or Xbox games lying around, we would use the boxes for bats. A big group of us would be sprinting around a table in a tight room, using these Xbox game boxes, some of the lads with hotel slippers on. It was an absolute recipe for disaster, but it always kept us entertained.

We play a lot of pool at the training ground. It's always good playing against Matt McCann, the press officer, because he'll get into a great position and then the pressure will get to him and he'll lose his head. Everyone loves watching Matty lose his head . . . We always played a lot of darts when we were away with England at tournaments. It was good for morale and team spirit. Not everyone wants to be playing games all the time, so obviously you respect that, but it's good for bonding if there is a group of you doing things together and having fun during your downtime. When you're away a lot, you need to have people who are ready to enjoy being away and enjoy being in each other's company. Doing stupid stuff like that helps.

As the record appearance holder for the England under-21s, what are some of the stories and craziest experiences you had whilst playing for the Young Lions? @tomhwilliams23

A lot of it was similar to what I've just mentioned, but I can also remember lots of stupid challenges. There was a Jacob's Cream Crackers challenge where we had to try to eat as many as we could in two minutes without having a drink. Then there was the Weetabix challenge – try to eat two dry Weetabix in a minute. (It's not as easy as it sounds. The secret is not to put loads in at once. You've got to go little and often. Don't try it at home, kids.) Or drinking bottles of water as quickly as we could. I can remember Scott Carson being sick off his balcony. In fact, I can also remember David Nugent sprinting down the hotel corridor in flip-flops with a fire axe in his hand. That's one of the images that really sticks in my mind from my under-21 days. If the staff had seen any of this, they would have gone mad.

I know it's stupid, really childish stuff, but it was just young lads away, being bored. You didn't have Netflix back then. You didn't have Sky everywhere you went. There wasn't much available, so a lot of the time we had to make our own entertainment.

We used to amuse ourselves in other ways. There would be a lot of meetings and sometimes the FA would want to use us as guinea pigs to trial things they weren't ready to roll out with the seniors. We were all told to supply urine tests and I remember David Bentley filling his sample bottle with apple juice. The guy was going mad. 'How is your reading like this? I don't understand. You should be dead.'

We were young lads and it wasn't easy being away for so long and just confined to your hotel. Often we were bored out of our minds. I remember on one trip Scott Carson saying: 'Is there any chance of us getting an afternoon off? I just want to go out and see some . . . civilians.' That cracked me up and I knew exactly how Scott felt. He wasn't talking about women or anything like that. He just meant wanting to see some normal human beings, rather than everyone you see being a footballer or football team staff.

That is genuinely an issue on those long international breaks. St George's Park is a really impressive place, with great facilities, but it often used to feel that there was no escape from football after training. Every picture in your room is football-related. Every bit of space in the whole place is dedicated to football. I preferred when England stayed at the Grove down south because it was a normal hotel, all the facilities were great, good food, golf course, everything I need to keep me happy, and it was all just a bit more chilled out. You're there for work, but I think you need time to switch off after training rather than seeing football, football, football everywhere you look.

Do you agree with those who say there is too much football?

There's definitely too much. It's not just the number of matches: it's the way they're scheduled; it's the way the schedule carries on all year round, with almost no break between one season and the next. That's one of the reasons why I retired from international football. It's just so much football and so little time to relax and recharge the batteries at the end of the season before it all starts up again.

Our manager was talking recently about the demands put on Sadio Mané, who, as he put it, had a 13-month season by the time he had finished playing for Senegal at the Africa Cup of Nations. He and Mo were playing at that tournament while we were in pre-season training. They only managed to get a short break before the new season started. Alisson and Bobby were both in the Brazil squad for the World Cup last year, then had a brief holiday before the season started, then played the whole season for Liverpool, finishing with the Champions League final on 1 June, and then it was straight to the Copa América. Again, that leaves you with only a short break before going straight into the new season when mentally, as well as physically, you need time to switch off.

The whole thing has got to be looked at. There shouldn't be major international tournaments every year. It should be World Cup one year, then a summer off, then the continental tournaments – the Euros, the Copa América, the Africa Cup of Nations and so on – then a summer off, then the World Cup again. The reason they won't do that is because they want them all to be on at different times so they can get the biggest TV audience possible, but I think most players would say they should be all in the same summer, ideally all around the same time, and players should be playing in tournaments every other year rather than every year. Otherwise you're just flogging the players year after year and it's going to have a serious impact on careers. How long can you realistically be expected to play 60 or 70 games a season without breaking down?

Not only that, but I'm sure the quality suffers when players are turning up at these tournaments exhausted at the end of a long, hard season. People ask why certain players aren't at their best during World Cups. A lot of the time, the answer is pretty obvious. They're exhausted. If you're training for the Olympics or the Tour de France or the Grand National or whatever, you're gearing all your training towards peaking at that precise time. In football you don't have that luxury. It's a year-round sport and you have to be on it every week. Then you get to the end of the season and, oh, it's the World Cup. I don't think it's a surprise when sometimes the quality suffers at those tournaments or when players find it hard to produce the kind of performances that we're used to seeing at club level.

It's a strange thing about football. The top players are expected to be at the same level week after week, season after season, for their whole career. When they have a little dip in form, people are, like, 'What's going on? What's happened to him?' And it could be a number of things – something behind the scenes at their club, something going on in their personal life – but ultimately it's natural for players to have dips in form every now and then. Sometimes you feel amazing physically and mentally. Sometimes you get to 70 minutes and you're having to slog your way through. You're asking players to be on top of their game every week, every month, every year, and it's not realistic when you're playing all year round. They should do more with the fixtures and the tournaments to ease the workload, but if anything they seem to be going the other way, with talk of more and more new tournaments. As ever, money talks.

Match Day:
Half-time

On the stroke of half-time, Klopp always sprints to the dressing room. What's his half-time ritual? @kirchlin

With some managers, you'll walk into the dressing room and the manager will start screaming and yelling straight away – and that can happen when you're winning too. Fabio Capello was probably the most extreme I've come across for that. He could explode and go from zero to 100 in an instant. Some players come off the pitch steaming. Danny Mills was a big one for that when I was at Leeds. Wayne Rooney was capable of a head-loss in the dressing room when things weren't going well.

Our gaffer at Liverpool will certainly let us know about it when we're not performing, but it tends to be calm when we first reach the dressing room. All the gaffer wants to know at that point is whether anyone has had a knock or they're struggling. If so, he'll want them examined by the medical staff. One or two of the subs might be sent out to warm up, just in case. Then the gaffer will spend a few minutes in deep discussion with his coaches. There's a separate room for them to do that at Anfield. At smaller away grounds, it might just be in one corner of the dressing room. At this point, some of the players will be talking among themselves, but it's fairly quiet. One of the forwards might be pointing out how much space he's getting if one of us can find him. The defenders might be pointing out that they need more help in certain situations. But it's small conversations rather than anyone screaming and yelling. If anyone needs to be strapped up or to change their boots or go to the toilet, that's the time for it.

I always change my shirt at half-time. If it's pouring down with rain, I'll change my whole kit. If there are any injuries, dead legs or things like that, the staff might bring an exercise bike through so that you can keep your legs moving when the manager comes back in to do his team-talk.

Capello's team-talks were pretty extreme. One that sticks in my mind is just before the World Cup in South Africa, when we played a warm-up game against a local team in Rustenburg. We had two different line-ups – one to play the first half and one to play the second – and we were expected to win comfortably. I was playing in the second half and at half-time it was still 0–0 and the lads weren't playing well. We were all fearing the worst, but then Capello started by saying, calmly, 'Yes, it was a good first half. You did everything I asked you to do.' The lads were looking around thinking, 'Okay, that's not what we were expecting, but we'll take this.' And then he just exploded, off the scale, yelling, 'No, you f***ing DIDN'T.' He smashed his hand down on the table in front of him and absolutely went off on one. At that point I had to go out and warm up for the second half, which was probably a relief: I was thinking, 'Well, at least we can't do any worse than they did in the first half.' Yes, Fabio's half-time team-talks could be quite lively.

Our gaffer can get very animated on the touchline and he's certainly capable of flying off the handle when he has to, but a lot of the time in the dressing room he's calmer than people might imagine. When he and his staff come through after their chat, a lot of what he says to us will be about videos that the analysts have prepared. In our dressing room at Anfield we've got a big screen that he can use for those presentations. Some away grounds will have the same facilities, but at other grounds the staff will bring through this portable pop-up projector thing. They'll have tape on the floor for the exact place where they need to put it. In some of the tighter away dressing rooms, it's ridiculous, having all of us huddled around this projector.

The manager will usually show us a few different clips to back up the key messages he wants to get across. It might be to tell the defence, 'You're not high enough. Move up to here,' or it might be something about set-plays or he might just tell us all that we need to do more of a certain thing – or less of a certain thing – when we're building up possession. He might show us how a certain type of attack or cross is working and another type isn't. A lot of players respond better if they can see something demonstrated on a screen. He's very clear in the way he communicates with us.

Some managers fly into an absolute rage. Some managers rarely raise their voice. Some managers raise their voice all the time, just to try to get a reaction. I've seen other managers who, when they know the end is coming, have not really known what to say, so a senior player has had to step in. Then there was the manager who just walked in at half-time, said 'Play better second half' and walked out again. As I recall, we did play better in the second half and we won the game. I suppose that manager might say his team-talk was inspirational. I think most of the players would have a different view.

What kind of team-talks do you give to lift the morale of the players? @_venyy

'Dirty' team-talks, according to the manager in a recent interview! I'm guessing what he means by that is that if there needs to be a rallying cry when we're in the dressing room, it's probably easier for someone like me to say those things than it is for him to say them in his second language. His English is pretty much perfect, but if he wants me to say certain things in a certain way, then, as a senior player, I'm happy to do that. I've been around football a long time, working under a lot of different managers, and I can probably gauge the mood – when it's the right time for strong words and when it's the right time for something a little more subtle. I'll think about what we've worked on tactically in the build-up to the game and I'll try to reflect that too.

Mind Games

What's the source of your motivation, champ? @wegoagain17

In a word, winning. I have to win at everything I do. I'm a terrible, terrible loser. Shocking. Whatever I'm doing, I want to be the best at it. Or the best I can be.

Another motivation, related to that, is the desire to prove people wrong. That has always been a big one for me. Throughout your career, you're always going to have people who don't rate you. Even Messi and Ronaldo will have people who try to pick apart their achievements or their performances. You're always going to be liked by some people and not by others. If someone says 'James Milner isn't good enough,' it's a big thing for me to try to prove them wrong and shut them up.

I've always been like that, really – desperate to prove people wrong, desperate to do the best I possibly can, to win every match I play, to win trophies and, yes, desperate not to lose. I've heard various sportspeople say that the defeats stay in their minds longer than the victories. I would agree with that. Both times we won the Premier League at City, it was straight into a tournament with England afterwards and that feeling of joy didn't really last as long as it should have done. If we'd missed out on the title that year, I think that would have eaten away at me the whole time I was away. That's how it felt when we lost the Europa League final at the end of my first season at Liverpool and then I was away for a month at the Euros with England, barely getting a kick. I dwelt on that defeat for a long time. That was more fuel for the fire.

Then when we were beaten by Real Madrid in the Champions League final in 2018, again it was a motivation. That didn't leave me all summer. Going back to pre-season training about five weeks later, walking through reception and seeing the board with the club's roll of honour – and it was still five European Cups, not six – that just made me even more desperate to win a trophy for the club. When you play for a huge club like Liverpool and you see all the history, it's obviously a small achievement just to be part of that. You have to earn the right to play for the club but also, once you're there, you've got to earn the right to be part of its history. The only way to do that is by adding to that great history by winning a trophy. I was desperate to win something the following season, even more eager than ever, and thankfully we did. And it was great to walk into Melwood for pre-season and see that the number of European Cups had been updated from five to six. But the number of league titles was still 18, not 19, and that is what we want to change.

The memory of winning trophies lasts for ever – and winning the Champions League with Liverpool certainly will, as will the celebrations in the city the next day – but when your career is unfolding day by day, that buzz and those feelings of joy and sheer happiness really don't last long before you have to reset and start to focus on the new season. There isn't time to stop and admire your achievements when you're still playing. The time to do that is when you've retired, although hearing the chants of 'We are the champions, champions of Europe' is always nice.

How hard is it when you're not being picked?

Again, it's horrible. You train all week, at 100 per cent, flat out, and then the weekend comes and you're not allowed to do your job. Even at this stage of my career, having worked under a lot of different managers, I still don't find it easy to accept that. There have been times when I've found it unbearable. When you know you're working hard and giving everything in training, giving everything for the team, performing well when you get the chance, and you're not playing, that is really difficult to take.

I was left out for the Champions League final against Tottenham. It goes without saying that I was desperate to start, having started pretty much every game in the competition, including both legs against Porto and both legs against Barcelona. We generally work on team shape a day or two before matches, which is when you get a pretty clear picture of what the line-up is going to be. With the final, there was a three-week build-up once the Premier League season was over, which meant we were working on team shape a lot earlier, and I think it was quite obvious from an early stage that the manager was planning to go with Hendo, Fabinho and Gini as his three in midfield. I can't pretend I was happy at the thought of missing out. Any player would be desperate to play in a Champions League final.

I actually found that the long build-up helped me get my head around it, though. Obviously I still hoped to persuade the manager to pick me and I needed to be ready in case one of the other lads got injured, but I was able to focus on doing a job for the team – even if it wasn't quite the job I wanted.

A lot of it comes down to the way the manager handles it. The manager can make it more bearable – or a lot worse. That's where you see the difference between a good man-manager and a bad man-manager. It's very frustrating when a manager, who has been a player himself, doesn't seem to appreciate how it would feel to be left out without an explanation. You always prefer a manager who is willing to have those difficult conversations. Otherwise you just start questioning yourself. Why is it? What could I be doing differently? Does the manager not rate me? Does he just hate me? Is he taking me for granted because he thinks I'll just accept it?

Different players deal with rejection in different ways. Some just shrug because it doesn't really matter to them or because they've given up trying to convince the manager. Some go the opposite way and rant and rave, or they kick up a stink in training. I'm glad we haven't got any of that type at Liverpool. I have always taken the attitude that, if I'm being left out of the team, I need to get my head down and work even harder. That is definitely the right approach, but I also think it has worked against me at times in my career under certain managers. If it was a choice between me and another player, and I was likely to take it on the chin and just focus on what I could do to affect the game from the bench – no tantrums or falling out – whereas the other player was likely to go banging on doors or mouthing off or kicking up a stink in the dressing room, then which is the easier choice for the manager? It has definitely felt at times like leaving me out was the easy option for certain managers. It's incredibly frustrating when that happens.

What is the hardest thing about playing football? What is the thing you dread most during the season? @Laurenballewske

I really hate not playing and I *really* hate losing, as I've said elsewhere. I know much worse things happen in life, but that feeling after you've lost, or the day after that, is just horrible and it's one I won't miss in the slightest when I retire. The thing I dread most is pre-season training. I won't miss that either.

But the most difficult thing of all, in some ways, is when you're injured. It's horrible. Some people might look at it and think, 'Well, you're getting paid X amount. It can't be that bad.' But as a professional footballer, you want to be playing all the time. Ask pretty much any footballer and they'll tell you that they hate watching. You try to offer as much support as you can in the dressing room beforehand, but when you're injured you feel like you're letting everyone down. When you're watching a match, you feel like you should be out there helping them. If the team are doing badly, you want to get out and help them and you feel guilty that you can't. If they're playing well and getting results, that's great, but you don't feel like you're contributing to it. Being injured is a horrible time.

Touch wood, I've been fairly lucky with injuries. I've never had a really bad one. I've played through a lot of injuries when I probably shouldn't have done, but I've never been out for a year or anything like that. The worst one I've had was when I was playing for Newcastle in 2008. I did it at Anfield. I went to clear the ball down the line and Lucas Leiva came in with his studs up and I followed through and kicked him, which broke my foot. I thought that was a bit of a naughty one from Lucas and it was one I didn't forget, but I got to know him when I moved to Liverpool and he was a really great lad, so I crossed his name out of my little black book.

Anyway, that happened in early March and I didn't play again for the rest of the season. We were battling to avoid relegation at the time, which just increased that sense of feeling like I was letting people down by being injured. I tried to rush back and I started having pain in another part of my foot. I tried to ping a ball in training and it left me in sickening pain. The medical staff said: 'Go and have this steroid injection, go away on holiday and you'll be fine when you come back.' I was really nervous about it because I had to take that whole summer off, waiting for it to heal, and I wasn't even able to try it out. If it had flared up when I came back, I would have been back to square one, having wasted the whole summer. Luckily it worked and I was fine for the start of that season.

But being injured is horrible. Your working day is completely different from the rest of the squad. You're in at different times and you might be in a different part of the building and not see your team-mates. Depending on just how bad you feel, that might be a relief. But it's a lonely existence and it takes good team-mates around you to keep your spirits up. Some players don't want to be around the team when they're injured because it makes them feel even worse, like they're letting their team-mates down by being injured. It doesn't really make sense, because nobody is to blame for being injured, but I can understand why people feel that way.

What does it take to come back from long-term injury?
@Talkingred23

As I've said – touching wood again – I've been lucky not to have had any really bad injuries, but when that happens, you need to set yourself goals – short-term, medium-term, long-term. You can't try to force it too quickly. If you're only focused on the long-term goal, you might lose sight of what you need to do day-to-day. Try to turn the negative into a positive. Think how you might be able to come back a better player by working on other parts of your body to make you stronger in other areas. Danny Ings did his cruciate in his first training session under Jürgen Klopp. It was the second time he had done it and he approached it in a fantastic way, setting himself little targets. Rather than 'swimming today' or 'bike today', he and the staff would, say, talk about him cycling from Liverpool to Rome – however many miles it is – or swimming the Channel over a certain stage of his rehab. These are just little things to make those sessions a bit more fun rather than it simply feeling like yet another bike session. You can race against people online now, with the modern equipment, and again, that helps to keep it interesting. You start on crutches and your first goal is to be able to walk without them. Then you're in the gym and you want to be able to run outside again. Then you're running in a straight line again, then you're starting to twist and turn, then it's ball work and then, eventually, back to full training. It can be a long, gruelling and very lonely process, so it's about showing the mental strength to stay focused on the day-to-day targets, which in turn brings you closer to the longer-term goals. Otherwise it can feel like groundhog day.

If there's a team-mate there with you, going through the same thing, obviously you don't wish that on anyone, but it can make the process easier to bear. Joe Gomez and Ingsy went through it together with their cruciate. Some days you're going to come in feeling incredibly low, but the other guy can help pick you up – and vice versa when they're feeling low. You can help each other to stay positive. That's massively important.

It's ridiculous to feel that you're letting people down by being injured, because it's not your fault, but you can't help it because you want to be out there helping your team-mates, helping the club, performing for the fans. And then on top of that, if you've been out for a long time, you've got people criticising you for being injured and referencing your wages. One line you'll hear – and maybe this is more of a social media thing – is 'We're not paying your wages to sit in the treatment room.' It drives me mad when I hear that kind of thing.

I've been with team-mates in social situations when people have come up to them and said something jokey about them being injured all the time. Footballers can take a joke about most things, but not that. When you're injured and you're working so hard to try to get fit, and you're not able to do your job and you feel guilty, and it seems like there's no light at the end of the tunnel, it really isn't a laughing matter.

No one wants to be injured. Being injured, on the side-lines, is just a horrible feeling. And it doesn't happen out of choice. It happens when players put their bodies on the line to play for a club. Yes, they still get paid by the club, but no players worth their salt are thinking about that when they're injured. It's no consolation whatsoever. I've seen so many players who have had their careers damaged or ruined by putting their bodies on the line to play for a club, often because their manager wants them to rush back before they're ready. That might damage your career, reduce your earnings or force you to retire early. And even when you're fit again, if you've been out for a while, it can take a long time to get back into the rhythm. It's not just like picking up where you left off. It can take weeks or months to build up your sharpness again. Some people never get back to the same level. I know it's frustrating for fans when they see a player injured, but believe me, it's 100 times worse for the player.

You have an amazing ability to remain fit and avoid injuries. Is that down to a bit of luck and eating healthily? Or are you working with backroom staff on load management? If so, do all the players do this? @task_jon

It's a combination of factors. There's definitely an element of luck. I've had tackles that could very easily have broken my leg if the timing had been a split second different. There was one really bad one from John Terry when I was playing for Villa in the FA Cup semi-final against Chelsea. There have been lots of others where I've had potential leg-breakers and I've been lucky. I have picked up plenty of smaller injuries over the years – I'm often nursing a knock or a strain of some sort – but I've been fortunate not to get any really serious ones. Touch wood, touch wood, touch wood.

I've not had too many muscle injuries – again, touch wood. Is that down to the way I've been built? It might be a factor, I don't know. I certainly think the work I do in the gym has helped to strengthen my muscles and maybe that has built up my resistance to certain types of injury. As you get older, you get to know your body. You start to be able to work out when it's just something you can play through without it getting worse and when it's something that needs a bit more careful handling.

And then, as you suggest, there's the work that the clubs do on the sports science to help you manage your workload. They look very carefully to track how much running you're doing in each game, at what intensity and so on, and they know, from all the data they have from all the tests, when a player is heading towards the 'red zone' when the risk of injury grows. No player likes to be told he needs a rest, but at Liverpool the staff are very good at spotting potential problems before they arise.

Players pick up knocks all the time, but the medical staff know how to treat them. As an example, I got a whack on my left knee when we played Chelsea in the Super Cup final in August. That was the Wednesday night and it could easily have put me out of our game at South-ampton on the Saturday lunchtime. I had an ice pack on my leg as soon as I went to the bench. After that, I used two different compression treatments. One of them, which is called Game Ready, uses ice and cold water to provide compression through a wrap that went around my knee. It's said to be developed with NASA space-suit technology. On the flight back from Istanbul the next afternoon, I used another compression treatment called NormaTec, which helps to enhance the blood flow around the injured area. A few of the lads used that on different knocks. There's a limit to how much a good compression treatment can do, but it does seem to work wonders for recovery. I was fit to start at Southampton on the Saturday lunchtime, which had seemed unlikely when I boarded the flight from Istanbul 48 hours earlier.

There are other little things that have probably worked in my favour over the years. Wearing studs, rather than blades, is one of them; if a blade gets caught in the ground, it stays where it is as your knee twists, whereas a round stud will usually rotate with your body. I've always worn round studs for that reason. I also wear a carbon plate in my boot to help me with a foot problem I had earlier in my career.

All these little things have helped, I think. But if someone piles into you at pace and your studs get caught in the ground, then it's going to come down to luck and split seconds of timing. No one is safe from that – which is why I'm touching wood like mad right now.

Does your job ever get boring? I know that you're doing what you love and are well paid for it, but surely there must be times where you feel you could do without it. @BaldyPaul

It's very rare that I feel like that. I'd say that 99.9 per cent of the time I enjoy it. But inevitably, over the course of a long career, there will be moments when we forget how lucky we are. That might not be what fans want to hear, when you're getting paid well for doing something anyone would love to do, but when it's your job, and you're doing it day after day, week after week, year after year, you're not always going to go to work – and it is work – with a spring in your step.

I love being a professional footballer and it has given me some unbelievable experiences and given me a lifestyle I couldn't have dreamed of when I was growing up, but yes, there are times in everyone's career when it's no fun at all. When you're at a club that is going through a difficult patch, or if you're injured or you feel like you're out of favour with the manager, that's tougher than people might realise. I know people will say, 'Yeah, but you're getting paid X amount a week,' but unless you're the type of person who is only motivated by money, you're not going to think like that.

The big challenge is to stay motivated through all of it, through all the ups and downs you have in your career. It's why you have to take your hat off to people like Ryan Giggs, Steven Gerrard and Frank Lampard for going as long as they did at the very highest level and retaining the hunger to win things year after year. It's not as easy as it might sound.

Have you ever had dark thoughts or suffered with social anxiety or depression? If so, how did you overcome this and how did people around you react? @Syd_Blease

I've had great highs in my career, but there have also been times when I've felt incredibly low. I can remember going home in tears when I was at City because I felt so low – not just the usual frustrations that you can have from one week to the next, but feeling utterly despondent because I was training really well and playing really well and I was still being left out week after week, and I felt there was nothing more I could do. That might sound totally trivial and I'm sure some people will point out that Premier League players are getting paid a lot of money to do a job that most people would love to do, but when so much of your self-esteem is based on playing at the weekend, it really is very hard to take being rejected week after week. If you weren't ambitious and driven, and you *were* more interested in what you were being paid, I'm sure it would be a lot easier. But that's not what most players are like.

It's not always easy to know what is classed as depression and what isn't. I've had team-mates who have had real difficulties, whether it's dealing with long-term injuries or other issues, such as alcohol or gambling or their marriage breaking up. Sometimes you can't even tell what they're going through at the time. I've sometimes heard things afterwards and thought, 'Shouldn't I have noticed?' But a football club dressing room is one of those workplaces where people don't really like to show any sign of weakness. Maybe those few hours they're at training are the one time in the whole day that they're able to put on a brave face and get on with things – and then as soon as they get into the car for the drive home, they're struggling again.

That drive home is difficult when you're raging, with

everything going through your head. It's difficult for your family if you come home in a dark mood, particularly for your wife. But having your family around you helps. It must be harder for those players who are going home to an empty house, particularly those who don't have friends or family nearby.

Players don't live in each other's pockets away from the pitch these days, so you're less likely to know what's going on in someone's life and you're probably not as likely to be really close to your team-mates as players once were. If someone is going through dark times, they might not find it easy to turn to their team-mates. As a team-mate, you might be none the wiser if they're just coming into training, keeping themselves to themselves and quietly trying to get on with things. There are a lot more resources within football these days, but I still think a lot of players would find it very difficult to say that they're struggling. It's hard in any walk of life, but I suspect it's even more so in professional sport, where the attitude is that you've got to be mentally strong and grit your teeth and get on with it.

Everyone goes through difficulties at some time. It might be bereavement or problems in their relationship or with their children, or it might be mental health difficulties. In some jobs, you would be given as much time as you needed. As a professional footballer, it's hard to take time off in a situation like that. You might not even want to tell anyone about it because it might feel – wrongly – like admitting a weakness. And then, on top of that, you might have people abusing you on social media when you're already feeling on the edge.

In football, it can seem like there's no hiding place for a player who is going through a hard time. I think it's easy for people to forget that footballers and any other high-profile figures are human beings. No matter how successful they might be, or how much they get paid, they aren't immune from struggles in their personal lives.

Team-mates:
Part Two

What happens when the relationship between a player and the manager turns toxic?

I've seen it at some of the clubs I've played for. Some of the cases were pretty well documented, like the flare-up at Newcastle, where Graeme Souness accused Craig Bellamy of refusing to play on the wing against Arsenal at Highbury – and then Bellers got off the bus and immediately did a TV interview, saying the exact opposite. There was the one at City, where Carlos Tevez had a huge falling out with Roberto Mancini. Did he refuse to come on as a sub at Bayern Munich in the Champions League? I was one of the ones who was next to Carlos at the time and I'm still not sure of what he said. (Incidentally, what a player Carlos was. Absolutely superb.)

I've seen hundreds of fallings out between managers and players, and it's never good, but when it gets personal and it starts to affect the rest of the squad, that's a different matter. It often becomes a stand-off. It can be tough when it's a player who's a big character in the dressing room, where players get along with each other. The player often ends up exiled from the group, training with the reserves or whatever. That's never a good situation to be around.

I remember, at one club, a player being exiled by the manager. He was then invited back to train with us again and he would just mess up the session on purpose. We would be doing a shooting drill, where you had to knock a diagonal ball out to the wing and then move infield and try to get on the end of the cross. First of all he would hit his diag 30 yards over the coach's head. Then the coach would knock the ball to him and he would take a touch and then just smash it in the other direction, over the fence, and the rest of us were left just looking at him in disbelief.

It can get to the point where the manager is desperate to get rid of the player – and the player is desperate to get rid of the manager. It's as if the player thinks, 'I'm going to kick up a stink until this manager has gone.' That's the last thing you want happening in your dressing room.

It's one of the biggest clichés in football, but can a manager really 'lose the dressing room'?

Yes. It can happen. It probably shouldn't, because as players we should all be capable of giving 100 per cent every day no matter what. But we're human beings. So are managers. Usually, when a manager first takes over a team, he's strong, with a clear vision of what he wants to do, how he wants the team to play and how he wants everyone to behave. The very best managers don't lose that. They keep that authority over the dressing room. But with time, with defeats, with the media and the fans on their back, with pressure from the boardroom, some managers lose their way a bit and start to lose their authority over the dressing room.

Sometimes it's as if managers start to lose faith in what they're doing or they don't fully believe what they're doing any more. And you can tell. I've seen some managers become obsessed by what the media are saying about them, to the point where they mention it in every team meeting. That's never a good sign.

It's always a bit of a concern when a manager changes personality when he's under pressure. I've seen managers who are laid-back try to crack down on things they would usually let go. I've seen other managers, disciplinarian types, go the opposite way. And if the manager's standards are dropping, it's probably going to be the same with some of the players too.

As I said before, it's not something that should happen, but I'm sure there are similar patterns in a lot of workplaces in different industries, where a boss comes in, makes a big impression and a big improvement and then, over time, standards start to slip. Even if it just means two or three players slackening off by 5 per cent or 10 per cent, that can have a very negative impact.

A lot of it comes down to man-management. I've worked under some brilliant man-managers and the odd terrible one. Some don't treat their players with respect and, over time, that's not going to pan out well for them or the team. One of the lads at Liverpool told me about a manager who, the day after they lost a game, got the players together in training and told them to stand in formation. Then he blew his whistle and made them stand in those positions for 45 minutes. 'This is what you did yesterday, so this is what we're doing today.' Then he blew the whistle for half-time, changed ends and made them do the same again for another 45 minutes. Eleven players just standing there in silence, probably at risk of their muscles seizing up. I can see the point he was trying to make, but that's ridiculous. It would be hard for any group of players to respect a manager who treated them like that.

Everyone tries to be as professional as they can, but if relationships aren't good and it becomes an unhappy workplace, that can obviously have a negative effect on performance. I don't like the phrase 'lost the dressing room', but it's something that can happen, without anyone wanting it to.

*Have you had team-mates who, despite being talented foot-
ballers, don't like the game?*

For some players, it probably feels like it's just a job to
them. I'm sure they enjoyed it as a kid, but maybe once they
become a full-time professional, they come across things
they don't like. Maybe they liked playing for fun but don't
like the seriousness and intensity of it when it becomes their
full-time job. Some won't like the training or the travelling
and some will find that the game causes them such lows
that they just don't love it any more. A lot of people find
the scrutiny and the pressure too much. They love playing,
but they don't like being in the public eye.

I can only think of one player I've played with – I'm not
going to name him – who genuinely gave the impression
he was only interested in picking up his money. He had had
a few injuries and didn't really seem too bothered about
trying to get fit again. Whether he really didn't care, I don't
know. Maybe it was just bravado. It's not easy to know what
pushes a player to the point where they feel like they don't
care any more. It's the kind of attitude that would frustrate
me enormously as a team-mate, but you don't always know
what's going on in someone's life.

Everyone is driven by different things. Most people want
to be the best player they can possibly be, to reach the
highest level they can and to win trophies. Some people
might be more interested in individual acclaim than team

success. Some just want to be rich or famous and football is the way they can achieve that. They end up being more interested in the money and the fame than they are in the game that made them rich and famous in the first place. Everyone is driven by different things.

What's the story behind the old-man-walking-stick celebration? @darryl_dmello

It was just because Virg had been going on about me being the old man of the team, giving me a lot of banter, calling me 'grandad' and things like that. If there's a game from the 1970s on TV, Virg will screw his face up and be looking at it and then he'll say, 'Which number are you, Milly?' So I thought, 'Next time I score, I'll do the old-man routine.'

I'm usually quite old-school in my celebrations, but I've done a few that the lads have asked me to – in-jokes and that kind of thing. I love seeing a good celebration. It's the best feeling in the world to score a goal and, at the end of the day, football is entertainment. People pay good money to watch football, whether in the stadium or on TV, and the celebrations are part of the entertainment. It annoys me when people are booked for 'over-celebrating'. If the referees are told they've got to book anyone who takes their shirt off, then yes, they've got to do it. But why are they being told to book people? You've got to look higher up at the people who make the rules.

I remember as a kid, copying that Chelsea celebration where Roberto Di Matteo and all his team-mates lay down like they were posing for a photo. There are loads of great celebrations on YouTube and some daft ones too. There's the bowling-ball one where someone bowls an imaginary ball and all his team-mates fall over like skittles. There's that team from Iceland who have done dozens of them, like the fishing one, which is brilliant. It would get pretty tedious if that kind of thing was happening every time anyone scored a goal, but it's good fun. People want to be entertained. They should just relax things a bit around celebrations and let people have a bit of imagination. And that's me saying that – an old man!

What's the best dressing room prank there has been at LFC?
@TheAnfieldTalk

Dressing room pranks have probably gone out of fashion at most clubs. Everyone is more sensible now, a bit more boring. If I think back to when I was at Leeds, the dressing room culture is so different. It was almost non-stop back then.

I've seen a lot of pranks in my time. Let's just say a few of them are probably best not mentioned in a book like this. There were a couple at Villa that I'm definitely not going to go into. But I'll give you a taste of a few of the sillier ones. At Leeds, I remember Michael Duberry bringing in some fish and stuffing them in the ceiling of the staff dressing room, which stank the place out. The physio used to get called 'Sausage Fingers', so the lads wrapped his whole car in sausages. The groundsman complained about rabbits at the training ground, so the lads bought a load of rabbits and put them in the gym, which was massive, and he had to try to chase them out. I can still see him now, trying to corner all these rabbits, with the lads in hysterics. I mentioned earlier about getting my gear cut up on my 17th birthday, which was like a rite of passage for a young player.

Wayne Rooney liked a prank. Jonathan Woodgate too. Woody is very funny, very sharp and he always had to make sure he had the last word. I remember one point at Newcastle where he and Michael Chopra were having a bit of a ding-dong where they were doing various things to each other. They kept moving each other's car, that sort of thing. Then Woody somehow got his hands on a load of grasshopper eggs, which he brought to training and hid in Chops's car. Eventually they hatched and started hopping around his car, driving him mad.

This one isn't a prank, but legend has it that there was this thing called the 50p game. It was before my time, but I believe they used to do it in the reserve games – at Leeds and at other clubs too – where one player would take a 50p coin onto the pitch and if you got touched by the player who had it, you had to take it. The coin used to get passed around during the game and whoever ended up with it at the final whistle had to buy all the drinks afterwards. How utterly ridiculous is that! Can you imagine that happening now, with all the cameras they have tracking every player? The movement at corners would be incredible. I'm just imagining them picking that up in the TV studios or in the analysis room at the training ground. I think you would be sacked. We have a laugh and we get on well, but it's no longer that very old-school atmosphere that there used to be. I'm sure there are some clubs where some wild things still happen, but not on the scale they used to.

Who is the most intelligent player you have played with?

There's this stereotype that footballers are stupid. It's totally wrong. Maybe some are, but there are loads of intelligent players. I would say the most intelligent I've played with is Vincent Kompany. Like a lot of players, he's multilingual, but what really stands out about Vinny is the way he's so knowledgeable and so passionate about so many subjects. You've probably seen his commitment to helping the homeless in Manchester, which is fantastic. He did a master's degree while he was playing for City and he was always reading economics books. He started learning Chinese at one point. I thought I was doing well by learning Spanish. I would love to learn another language, but Chinese is some challenge.

Simon Mignolet was probably the most intelligent at

Liverpool. He's another one who is multilingual and has a degree – in politics – and he has various business interests away from football, including a coffee brand. I know the image is that we all spend our whole time playing *Fortnite* and eating Nando's, but there are loads of players who spend their time studying or doing whatever else might interest them outside of football. Some players do music, fashion, property, charity work and various different things – whatever interests them. It's good if you have interests outside of football. You need that, especially when it feels like it's non-stop football, football, football. You have to be focused on your day job, but not so focused that you've got no escape from it. I've seen some players get criticised for having their own clothing brands or whatever, but as long as it doesn't take away from your football, it's healthy to have other interests.

Are you the diva of the Liverpool squad? If not, which lad is it? @CuratorRex

It depends what you mean by diva. When you're talking about a group of footballers, you might usually mean it in terms of being a bit flash or spending too much time in front of the mirror. That's definitely not me. I'm probably the opposite. But if you're talking about someone who will moan if things aren't just the way they want them, that probably is me. If people are late or the timings don't work or the kit or the facilities aren't what I'm expecting, then I'll be the first one complaining about it. Dejan is the same. He loves a good moan if things aren't perfect. Is that being a diva? Some might say so, but I would like to think it's just about being professional and having high standards.

If you're talking about vanity, well, there are quite a few guys who battle it out over the mirror in the dressing room. I'll leave you to try to guess which ones. You can probably work it out.

Your forward line at Liverpool – Bobby Firmino, Mo Salah and Sadio Mané. What are the three of them like, both on and off the pitch? Max Pearce

All three of them are brilliant. Bobby is so under rated. He has amazing ability and does unbelievable things. He works incredibly hard for the team, he's so composed on the ball and he can always find his way out of tight areas. Off the pitch, he's very chilled out, relaxed, always smiling, likes a joke, really nice guy and he just goes about his business. He's never in the treatment room. I described him as a 'machine' earlier – a top-quality, low-maintenance machine. He can chuck a few shapes too, as you can see from his celebrations.

Sadio is another very chilled out character. He's a joker too. On the pitch, he's quick, very strong – he spends a lot of time in the gym – and he's a great finisher. He's become more confident and is scoring more and more goals. He's another one who I think is an even better player than people realise and is very dedicated. He's very popular, although less so when he tries to put his music on in the gym. We like it when it comes on in the dressing room before the match, but it's not necessarily music you want to work out to . . .

And what can I say about Mo that hasn't been said before? He scores goals and makes things happen out of nothing. A classic example would be the goal he scored against Spurs at Anfield, when he wriggled through when it seemed impossible. I can't think of many players in the world who would have been able to do that, but he's someone who scores big goals in big moments. He's another who spends a lot of time in the gym. He's always trying to improve. He's so hungry for goals. He's not as loud as Sadio, but he likes a joke too. He has a lot of pressure on him because of the profile he has in Egypt and all over the world; there was a huge mural of him in Times Square before the World Cup. The way he handles that pressure and fame is so impressive.

Who is the team-mate who you thought would make the big time that didn't fulfil potential?

I could reel off a dozen players from when I was 15 or 16 who I thought would go on to play for England, but what you come to realise is that there's no such thing as a certainty to make it when you're that age. Wayne Rooney was as close as you can get to a certainty, given how good he was when I used to play against him at under-11s and under-12s, but even with everything that he had going for him, it might only have taken one injury or one setback or an off-the-pitch issue, or a lack of opportunity at the right time, and it could have been a different story.

I mentioned Luke Moore earlier and I would say that, of all of us who played in that England under-16 team, he was the one who seemed most likely to go on to play for his country at senior level. He was brilliant. He scored a hat-trick for England in the first Victory Shield game against Northern Ireland. Then he got into the Aston Villa team and he scored a hat-trick for them in the Premier League when he was only 19, which was when I was on loan there. Then he got a shoulder injury and was out for a long time. Villa signed another couple of forwards when he was out and, for whatever reason, he didn't really get another run in the team.

Luke went on to have a good career at various other clubs and I hope it doesn't sound like I'm calling him a wasted talent or anything like that, because I'm not. I'm just saying that he was an outstanding player at youth level and maybe if he hadn't got injured when he did, which was really unfortunate timing, or if he had had better luck at one time or another, he would have gone on to play for England.

Injuries are such a massive thing for any player, but particularly for a young player looking to establish himself. Michael Bridges was another one who got injured at the worst possible time, when he was playing so well at Leeds and probably pushing for the England squad. Dean Ashton was a similar story. Dean was outstanding when I played with him in the England under-21 team, scoring lots of goals in the Premier League. Then he got called up to the England senior squad, broke his ankle in the first training session and missed the whole of that season. He recovered, had a great season at West Ham, got back into the England squad, made his debut and then picked up another serious injury and barely played again before retiring at the age of 26. It was such a shame for him. How unlucky can you get?

Micah Richards had a really good career, but he was another one who would have been even more successful but for injuries. He was an unbelievable right-back when he first broke through – amazing in the air, so strong, so quick, so powerful, unstoppable going forward. I played with him for England under-21s and then we had a good combination going on the right-hand side at City. I would have the ball and I would just hear 'MILLS, I'M COMING THROUGH' and he would be like a steam train coming past on the overlap. I would just roll it down the outside and – bang – you weren't stopping him. That game where City won 6–1 at Old Trafford in the first title-winning season, he was amazing, like a machine. He played more games than Pablo Zabaleta that season. That's how good he was.

And then he injured his ankle playing for Team GB at the Olympics, then his knee ligaments and – the same old story – from that point on he was fighting a losing battle. He kept going into the gym every day, doing his rehab work, trying to get fit, and his knee just kept letting him down.

Jonathan Woodgate is another. He played for some great clubs, as well as for England, but, having played with him at Leeds (very briefly) and Newcastle, I would have him down as someone who would have won loads more England caps had he not been so unlucky with injuries. England had some great defenders around that time – Rio Ferdinand, John Terry, Sol Campbell, Jamie Carragher – and I honestly think he was the equal of any of them. Because of the injuries, I don't think people realise how good he was.

Serious question. Why have no gay male footballers come out? @Hunterrr50

I would guess the main reason is the whole clamour around the subject. It annoys me that the media make such a big thing of it. 'Who will be the first gay player in the Premier League?' A bookmaker started laying odds on it a few years ago, which was just ridiculous. That's just making it harder. Surely the point is that in 2019 someone should be able to come out and it *not* be a big deal. By making such a big deal of it before it has even happened, you're just discouraging people from doing it.

I've seen people on panel shows say that there might be an issue with team-mates if a player came out. I don't think there would be even the slightest issue. Do people honestly think a player would be picked on or shunned because he was gay? I can only speak for myself, but it wouldn't make even the slightest difference to me if a player was gay. I don't understand why it would make the slightest difference to anyone.

What would your life be like if you had never met Divock Origi? @jerry3089

Haha. I often stop and wonder that. What would anyone's life be like without Divock Origi? Would we have won the Champions League without him? Possibly not. His contributions against Barcelona in the semi-final and Spurs in the final were absolutely immense. Every player did his bit, and I really don't like to single anyone out, but we were all absolutely delighted for Div. It felt like almost every time we needed a big goal last season, he came up with it.

Within our squad, you probably couldn't get two more different characters than Div and me. We're polar opposites. You know what I'm like. Div, on the other hand, is just so relaxed. If we have a team meeting, most of us will be there well before. He is always the last to arrive – never late, or very rarely, but not more than 30 seconds before the meeting starts. And that has become such a familiar pattern that it helps everyone to smile and relax.

There are two sides to him really. He's a very intelligent

guy and speaks four languages fluently, and you can tell how committed and determined he is by the way he has forced his way back into the team at Liverpool. But away from the pitch he's just so incredibly relaxed, without a care in the world. If ever someone has left something on the plane or on the bus, it will always be Divock. 'Does anyone know who these headphones are?' 'Yep. They're definitely Div's.'

What would my life be like if I'd never met him? Probably a lot less fun. Seeing him can only help me chill out – relatively speaking. How can I be stressed if this guy is just floating around on Planet Origi, super-chilled, smiling, leaving a trail of his possessions behind him?

Sometimes when you speak to him in the dressing room, you're not sure if he's listening. 'Does he remember what the manager has been telling us all week? Does he even know who we're playing today?' And then he'll come on in a big game and he'll produce the perfect performance as a sub – and you think, 'Yes, he was listening after all.' But there is one thing I still need to ask Div. You remember the stoppage-time winner he scored against Everton in the Merseyside derby last December? Why did he rush to get the ball out of the net afterwards and run back to the halfway line? I genuinely believe he thought we still needed another goal to win the game. It wouldn't surprise me in the slightest. I'll ask him. I hope he remembers it.

Match Day: Second Half

It often looks like there's a certain amount of 'needle' between different players, as if there's some kind of feud that has carried over from previous games. Is there any opponent that you have an ongoing feud or rivalry with? Kai Watson

People will probably think it's Messi after the Champions League semi-final last season! But I couldn't have more respect for him. What an incredible player.

There are certain players I've had a number of tough games against – Zaha is one that springs to mind – and other players I've had a few niggles with, but there's nothing I would describe as a feud or a running battle. You remember certain things like a naughty tackle. You don't mind a hard tackle if it's honest, but when it's a bad one, that's harder to forgive. I had a bee in my bonnet a few years ago after one player nailed me with a bad tackle in a Premier League game. I can't be certain whether I missed the next game, but one thing I definitely missed was a golfing trip with Harty and Gaz. We'd booked it in advance and I had already paid my share, so they went without me. I was cursing that player for a while afterwards, but I'm not sure I ever played against him again and I can't say that any resentment really lingered for long. It wasn't something I thought about for a while until just now.

How did your beef with Messi start? @Alpha_Ayanda

I don't have a beef with Messi! He's an absolutely incredible player. In my eyes, he's the best there has ever been. He nutmegged me when I was playing for City in a Champions League game in 2015 – I believe the clip has had one or two views on YouTube – but he nutmegs pretty much every player he comes up against. Why would I take that personally?

I caught him with a heavy challenge at Camp Nou when we played Barcelona in that semi-final last season. He wasn't happy at all. When we went down the tunnel at half-time, I gave him a tap and said, 'Are you okay?' or something like that. And he went off on one. He was shouting '*burro*', which means 'donkey' but is also a general term in Spanish football for someone who goes around kicking opponents. I don't know if he realised I could understand Spanish, but he said, 'You did that because I nutmegged you.' I wasn't going to get into a debate with him – though it would have been good practice for my Spanish – so I just left him to it.

It was nothing to do with a nutmeg four years earlier, I can assure you. He's an incredible player, the best in the world, and he was playing well. If you give him room, you're going to be in trouble. You can't let players, particularly top players, have it all their own way against you. That challenge was never going to hurt anyone, but you sometimes need to let an opponent know he's not going to have it all his own way against you. I'm sure he has had an awful lot worse than that challenge.

Messi is a phenomenal footballer. Unbelievable. A totally different level. When you're playing against him, you're conscious the whole time that he could do something incredible, in a split second, to transform the game. You can't afford to let him show how brilliant he is. If you show him too much respect, he will do some serious damage.

When someone makes a bad challenge in Sunday League, all hell breaks loose. At professional level, the stakes are so much higher because one mistimed tackle could end your career and damage your livelihood, so how do you react if someone catches you with a really bad challenge?

I don't mind the hardest tackles in the world if they're fair. If someone comes through, gets the ball and takes me as well, I don't mind that. You just get up and get on with it. The tackles that bother me are the dangerous ones where players go in with their studs up and they don't care what happens as long as they don't get injured.

I would never go in to try to hurt someone. Yes, you want to let them know you're there, but that involves trying to win the ball cleanly. Sometimes you're not going to time it right. Sometimes it's unfortunate where the ball is bouncing and a touch takes the ball away and a player goes in over the top without meaning to, but I would never make one of those naughty challenges I'm talking about where you're putting an opponent at serious risk. Those challenges where they're almost stamping as they're sliding in, they're the ones I really don't like. They can be leg-breakers. They are the ones that make people angry.

One ridiculous, awful challenge was in our pre-season friendly against Sevilla in Boston this summer just gone. One of the young lads, Yasser Larouci, was dribbling through a crowd of Sevilla players and one of them took a huge, deliberate, blatant swipe at Yasser's shin. Yasser went off on a stretcher and was lucky he wasn't seriously injured. Their lad apologised afterwards and so he should have done. I called it a disgrace afterwards and I stand by that.

Another one that caused a lot of ill feeling at the time was in the 2018 Champions League final in Kiev, when Mo Salah dislocated his shoulder after getting caught in a tangle with Sergio Ramos. A lot of our supporters were furious with Ramos, because losing Mo was such a blow to us in that final, but as a professional I was inclined to give Ramos the benefit of the doubt. I think Ramos is a player who – how to put this? – will do anything to win. He's a brilliant defender, but there have been occasions when he has gone into challenges where you're left thinking, 'How has he not seriously injured someone there?' He goes in hard and at times he probably goes over the top. He certainly puts his elbows to good use at times. But with that particular one, with Mo, do you really go into a challenge in that way with the intention of damaging someone's shoulder? Do I honestly think he went in to try to do Mo? No, I don't. He has obviously tried to pull Mo down. Only Ramos knows whether anything more went through his mind at that time, whether he thought, 'I'm going to shake him up a bit,' or something beyond that. If I'm 100 per cent honest, I don't think he tried to pull Mo's shoulder out or anything like that. I don't think that's a challenge that you make in order to try to hurt someone. I didn't feel any great resentment or hatred towards Ramos afterwards. I was only interested in the result and how it happened and thinking about what might have been. The fact that we got to the final 12 months later and won it, at the second time of asking, meant that we were able to put the Kiev final behind us – especially Mo.

What's the worst refereeing decision you've ever seen?

There are some obvious ones that stand out. I've already talked about the one where they didn't give the goal when Frank Lampard's shot went over the line against Germany in the World Cup in 2010 and the one where Nemanja Vidić got away with a yellow card for bringing down Gabby Agbonlahor in the League Cup final the same year. Both of those still rankle.

But the weirdest refereeing decision, if I can call it that, was when Phil Dowd pulled me back during a game. I was running forward on the counter-attack and I sprinted past him, trying to get on the end of a cross, when I felt someone tug my shirt and then grab onto it. I looked around, thinking it was an opposition defender, and then I saw it was the referee, who was grinning to himself. He seemed to find it hilarious and, to this day, I've no idea what he was trying to do. Phil Dowd was also the one who didn't send Vidić off in 2010, so it's fair to say he wasn't my favourite ref.

Do you have much dialogue with refs during the game?

It really depends on the referee. Some like to have a constant dialogue with the players. Others say they're happy to communicate with you and then, when you try to engage with them, they completely ignore you.

I tend to think most of them do a good job in really difficult circumstances. They don't have to explain every decision. It's no good screaming at them. If anything, that's more likely to send them the other way. I think it's beneficial to try to have some kind of rapport with them, but as I said, some of them aren't interested in that.

What are your thoughts when you see players dive?

It's frustrating. When there's no contact whatsoever and someone throws himself on the floor, that's completely unacceptable. A line should be drawn under that. It drives me mad.

Where it becomes a bit more complicated is those instances where there's a foul and, realistically, the referee isn't going to give anything unless the player goes down. If someone fouls you in the penalty area – whether it's a shirt pull or a sliding challenge or anything else – and you stay on your feet, nothing tends to get given. If someone makes exactly the same challenge and you go down, you get a penalty more often than not. It might annoy you when a penalty is given against your team for that kind of thing, but if it's only going to get given if the player goes down, that creates a problem. Where is the incentive to stay on your feet?

Mo Salah was criticised in the media after we were given a few penalties last season, but if you take the one at Cardiff as an example, he had been pulled back and pulled back three or four times before he went down. It was clearly a foul, but he had to go down before the referee would give a penalty. I found it encouraging when the referee gave us a penalty against Arsenal this season when Mo was clearly pulled back by David Luiz. If that happens more often, players will feel they don't have to go down to win a penalty.

I think it would be better for everyone if referees felt confident enough to give fouls when a player stays on his feet. Tackling has to stay in the game – physical contact is fine as long as it's fair – but if a player is clearly getting pulled back three or four times like Mo was, referees have to be willing to give a foul based on the challenge, not on whether the player eventually goes down. The referees' job is so hard, but if they're waiting for players to go down, that adds to the problem.

Then there are those incidents where a defender is flying into a tackle and the forward, anticipating the contact, jumps out of the way so as not to get hurt. Is that classed as a dive? Hard to say. If a player is travelling at pace, it can sometimes take the slightest contact to knock him down. That might look like a dive, but is it? Again, it's hard to say. I'm not defending diving, because just chucking yourself on the ground to try to win a penalty or free kick is out of order and needs to be stopped, but it's not always clear.

What happens if you need the toilet during a game? Amy Goodison

Good question! You try to make sure you go for a pee beforehand. Once you start running, you generally don't need to. Because your hormone levels change during exercise, it can be very hard to produce a urine sample after a game, never mind during it.

As for . . . the other one, well, you hope it won't be an issue, but I've witnessed it when players have had a bad stomach or whatever. I remember when I was playing for Newcastle at Wigan, there was a break in play and Scotty Parker just sprinted off the pitch, past the manager and down the tunnel. I was thinking, 'Has he just been sent off? Have I missed something here?' What I had missed was that Scotty was desperate for the toilet and, with a break in play, he took the opportunity to run to the dressing room. Then he was straight back out again a couple of minutes later and getting on with the game.

In the worst cases, they won't manage to do that. There was an instance before my time at Leeds, where one player was walking awkwardly as he left the pitch at full-time. The physio asked him if he had done his hamstring or something.

'Erm, no. I've . . .' The player explained what had happened. Not good, but it can happen. If you're playing Sunday League in your local park, you can run off and go behind a tree or something. It's not so easy to be inconspicuous when you're in a stadium full of people.

What's the strangest match you've ever played in?

I didn't actually play in it, because I was on the bench, but I think the strangest game I've been part of was when Newcastle played Villa at St James' Park in my first season there. It was just bizarre. Well, for 75 minutes it was a run-of-the-mill Premier League game. And then it went all a bit odd.

We were 1–0 down when Darius Vassell got through, took the ball around Shay Given and tried to knock it past Steven Taylor, who was on the line. It was going in, but Tayls stuck his hand out to block it. It was about the most blatant handball I've ever seen, even from 60 yards away on the touchline, but Tayls went down like it had hit his face, trying to convince the ref it wasn't a handball. I don't think he was the only player to have tried that trick, but the way he went down, I'm surprised he didn't rupture his spine. It was painful to watch. Anyway, the ref wasn't fooled. Tayls was sent off and Villa had a penalty, which Gaz Barry scored and we're 2–0 down and a man down with a mountain to climb.

Villa scored again, 3–0, and at that point I think most people inside St James' Park just wanted it to be over. I didn't because I was stripped off, ready to come on. Next thing I knew, two of my team-mates, Lee Bowyer and Kieron Dyer, started having a fight on the pitch. It was just near the halfway line, near where I was on the touchline, and the immediate thought was, 'What the *hell* is happening?' You quite often see players shoving each other on the pitch. You'll very occasionally see one player swinging at an opponent if he's really lost the plot. But that is the only time I've ever seen two players on the same team swinging at each other and fighting. Gaz Barry got involved and dragged them apart, but Bow and Kieron both got sent off and we were now down to eight men. 'Sit back down, James.'

From what I'm told, Tayls was in the dressing room feeling sorry for himself and couldn't work out what on earth was going on when the pair of them walked in. 'What's happened? Has the game ended already?' Bow and Kieron sat at opposite ends of the dressing room, neither of them saying a word. Tayls was still in the dark. Then apparently Kieron said something and it all blew up in the dressing room and they had to be separated again.

When I got to the dressing room at the end of the game, there was a stony silence and Alan Shearer walked in, knocked over all the recovery drinks which had been lined up and started yelling at Bow and Kieron. The recovery drinks went all over me – and at that time they were incredibly sticky, the kind of stuff you could probably have put wall-paper up with. Not great.

Then Graeme Souness came in and he just stood there, for what seemed like for ever, shaking his head in disgust, saying, 'Never . . . in all my years in football . . . Never have I ever seen anything as disgraceful as that.'

He must have seen all sorts of things over the years and had plenty of scraps himself, but never like that. He told Bow and Kieron they had to join him for the press conference and make public apologies in front of the TV cameras. That was the right thing to do, but of course we were all over the back pages for days after that. The media had a field day.

The strangest thing about the whole episode is that Bow and Kieron were good mates. There hadn't been any problem between them before that – and I don't think there was any problem after it either. It was just a really bad afternoon, 3–0 down at home, the fans unhappy, the players feeling the pressure and Bow, who could be feisty, got frustrated that Kieron didn't pass to him and it all just got totally out of hand. Maybe that gives you some idea of how pressurised it can feel on the pitch at times, when you're having a bad game and you're under pressure and it just takes one little thing for the red mist to start descending.

If managers want to switch formation or gameplan during a game, how is that information relayed? And how easy is it to adapt mid-match?

The gaffer will normally call one of us over during a break in play – usually Hendo or me because he knows we've got the biggest mouths. Then we just spread the words to make sure everyone knows, if we're switching to 4–2–3–1 or a diamond in midfield or whatever. We've been together a while as a team and we're usually fairly comfortable with changing formation if we need to. But it's not always easy because you rarely get a proper break in play. The important part is that everyone is made aware of it quickly. I've been in teams where you change system and half the lads think you're playing one formation and half the lads think you're playing another. I've experienced that with certain teams in the past. It's never good.

Usually it's something we will have worked on in training. Sometimes a manager might be in two minds before a game, working on two different systems in the build-up to the game, and he's prepared to flip from one to the other early on if it's not working. If he needs the personnel to be able to flip from one system to the other, the team selection might reflect that. As one of the players who can switch between different positions, I need to be aware of that.

Sometimes a manager will throw a curveball during a game, but I don't think I've ever seen one quite like the one

Stuart Pearce threw in at Man City that time when he put David James up front. It can't have been off the cuff because they had had an outfield shirt made with the number 1 on the back. I can understand the thinking behind it in terms of unsettling the opposition, but it's a pretty extreme approach.

What's your honest opinion about VAR, and would you and your team-mates want to see it used more or less than it is now? @Mister_TIBS

Honest opinion? I hate it. I worry that it's going to ruin football. The first time I experienced VAR was in an FA Cup tie against West Brom at Anfield. It gave us two decisions, but I still hated it. There was a three-minute delay before we were awarded a penalty and then a two-minute delay while they looked at whether one of West Brom's goals should have stood. Alan Pardew said afterwards that two of his players had picked up hamstring injuries because the stoppages were so long that they seized up.

Goal-line technology is brilliant – it takes a split second and you always get the right decision, yes or no – and I think there's probably something they could do technology-wise to get better decisions on offsides, but I can't stand VAR because even when the VAR and the referee have kept looking at an incident, you're still not getting a decision that everyone can agree on. If there were two of us looking at an incident, we could slow down the footage and watch a dozen times and we might still not agree on whether it's a handball, whether it's a dive, whether it's a red card, a yellow card or not even a foul. People are still debating the decisions with VAR, and when the game is being slowed down to such an extent, you have to ask whether it's really worth the disruption.

It works in other sports because the decisions are black and white. In cricket, was it going to hit the stumps or not? In rugby, was it a knock-on or not? In tennis, was the ball in or out? In those sports, 99 per cent of the time there's no debate once you see the video. In football the rules are a lot more subjective and I've always accepted that this means you're going to get inconsistencies because it comes down to one person's view of an incident. With VAR coming in, they've tried to make the rules more black and white, so we're now seeing penalties given for incidents that, in my opinion, should never be considered handball. Or we're seeing offsides given because, once they've watched it back a dozen times, someone is a fraction of an inch ahead of the defender when the ball is played. Is that what people want? It might be the right decision by the letter of the law, but, with the speed of the game, you're thinking, 'Seriously? Is it really worth slowing everything down and watching it again and again to give that decision?' And when the decision is still open to debate, it's even worse.

We've seen goals scored, then celebrated and then, after a two-minute delay, not given. Now we're going to have goals scored and then everyone is going to wait around while they look at the video and no one is going to celebrate because the moment has gone. That raw emotion, which is a huge part of why everyone loves the Premier League, is being taken out of the game. That's another big negative.

People who have played the game at any level understand that human error is part of football. Yes, we all get frustrated when there are poor decisions that cost our team, but I do honestly prefer human error. Football wasn't designed to be a robot game. I'm happy enough with goal-line technology because it's a black and white decision and you get the right situation immediately, but with VAR I just don't think the benefits are clear enough. They say that it will start to improve as everyone becomes more familiar with it, but I can't stand it. I'm fairly sure most players agree with me.

How much of the key to successful penalty-taking is practice, and how much is mental preparation? @gosulli

It's both. I always practise the day before a game – even if I'm not down for penalties, even if I'm not starting the game, because you never know what will happen. The analysts help us, providing information and videos which give us pointers about the opposition goalkeeper, whether he's more likely to go one way or the other, depending on your run-up, or whether he's the type who will commit himself early or wait until the last possible moment to decide which way to go.

When you've got all that information available, you study it carefully, just as you know the goalkeeper will be doing his homework about you.

My record is pretty good. Not perfect, but pretty good. You've got to be confident – know what you're going to do, believe in yourself. The important thing is that you handle the pressure. If I think back to the penalties I took late on against Fulham and Cardiff towards the end of last season, when we were going for the Premier League title, yes, you know the pressure is there, but you have to handle it. Physically, try to slow down your heart rate and try to manage the adrenalin and the nerves. Mentally, you have to stay calm, so that your only focus is on putting the ball in the net. Don't think about missing.

I've scored most of the penalties I've taken – including the two I mentioned against Fulham and Cardiff, and a big one for Liverpool against Paris Saint-Germain in the Champions League. One that felt huge at the time was the penalty to put Villa 1–0 up in the League Cup final against Manchester United at Wembley. There was that big one against Blackburn in the semi-final a few weeks before that, too.

For England, I scored twice in what felt like a never-ending penalty shoot-out against the Netherlands at the Euro under-21 finals in 2007. But I missed one in a shoot-out against Sweden at the same tournament two years later. I sent the keeper the wrong way, but unfortunately I slipped and it flew into the stand. I never took one for the England senior team. I would have fancied my chances of scoring in a penalty shoot-out, but I was substituted when we played Italy at Euro 2012. It was frustrating watching from the bench as we lost on penalties.

Funnily enough, one of those who scored for Italy in that shoot-out was Mario Balotelli, my team-mate at City at the time. Mario was so unpredictable on and off the field, but what a penalty-taker. Probably the best I've seen. He would take penalties in training all the time and he would drive Joe Hart mad. I said earlier that I prefer to decide where I'm going to put it and not change my mind, but Mario was the opposite. He would start his run-up and then he would just wait until the final moment. If Harty moved, he would put it in the opposite corner. If Harty didn't move, Mario would hit it hard enough, side-foot, that Harty couldn't get to it in time anyway. He was incredible. But the strange thing is that he went to AC Milan and missed two in the first few months there.

Penalties can feel like a bit of a lottery, but as with anything, the more homework you do and the more you practise, the better your chances. Find a technique you're comfortable with – whether that's power or precision, long run-up or short run-up, making up your mind early or waiting for the keeper to commit – and practise it.

And one last piece of advice: don't be terrified that you might miss. Even the best penalty-takers on the planet have missed one at some point. I just try to have something in mind and then to execute it. If I do that right and the keeper still manages to save, what can I do? That's what happened against Southampton when we were pushing for the top four late in the 2016/17 season. I hit the penalty well enough, but Fraser Forster, who had seen me take loads in training for England, made a good save. I was gutted at the time, but you just have to put it behind you. It can happen to anyone.

How far do you run in a match?

On average, I tend to run about 13km in 90 minutes, which is quite a lot when you consider how often a) play is stopped and b) you're not moving fast. Mine will usually be the highest in the team, but total distance covered is not the whole story. When you're playing football, it's very stop-start. There's a lot of high-intensity running in there and plenty of twisting and turning – plus accelerations and decelerations, which take quite a toll on your hamstrings and your other muscles. I remember playing one game for England in the Euro under-21 finals against the Netherlands in 2007, when we lost 13–12 on penalties. We effectively had nine men in extra time because we'd used all three subs, Nedum Onuoha went off injured and Steven Taylor was hobbling. It came up on the scoreboard afterwards that I'd done something like 18km in 120 minutes. I don't know if that's the most I've ever done, but as I said, it's less about the total distance than about what sort of running you're doing. In that game, it felt like a lot of the time was spent flat out, trying to prevent the Netherlands from making their advantage count.

Different players have different strengths. Mo and Sadio won't cover so much in total distance, but a lot of their running will be at high speed and high intensity. Bobby Firmino's work rate is amazing. Someone like Danny Ings would be a good example. He was always 'burst, burst, burst', a lot of sprints, trying to chase down the opposition and run the channels. Between those bursts, he would try to save his energy where possible.

My sprint distance won't be as high as some of my team-mates. But as a midfielder, I'll do more high-intensity running than most. I'm obviously – obviously – nothing like as fast as Mo or Sadio, but my average speed over the course of 90 minutes will usually be the highest in the team because I'm on the move for most of the game, whether we've got the ball or not.

Another important stat is the number of accelerations and decelerations you do over the course of 90 minutes. The more you do that – stop, start, sprint, stop, start, sprint – the bigger the load it puts on your hamstrings. When you're playing a pressing game, as we do, that load is heavy, so you have to be fit enough to handle it.

There are various devices and systems that clubs use, with cameras and GPS, to track your movement during training and during games. We wear GPS vests in training, but not in matches. The analysts have a very detailed breakdown of your physical performance in every game – not just to monitor your performance or your work rate but to keep an eye on your workload so that they can make sure you're not at increased risk of injury. Different players will have different levels for their 'red zones' and 'green zones'. If I run significantly less than 13km in 90 minutes, they'll try to find out why that is. Am I carrying an injury or was it just a more steady performance, which might be for tactical reasons? If I run 13km game after game, they know to look after me and handle my workload carefully – in training and in matches – over the next week or the next couple of games. I might need a down-day in training or be on the bike or do some jogging rather than being out on the training pitch. Some clubs give you the data as a matter of course. At Liverpool they tend not to do that, but they'll share it with you if they feel there's something you ought to know. Sometimes it's beneficial to let a player know if he's in that 'red zone'. At other times it's probably best if the player doesn't know. If you feel like you've had a heavy workload, you can potentially end up convincing yourself you're tired. They share the data on a need-to-know basis. That's a good approach.

How do players feel when they're substituted?

I can only speak for myself. Raging. Honestly, raging every time – even at my age, with a lot of miles on the clock! If you're 4–0 or 5–0 up, you're enjoying yourself and you want to keep going. If you're 1–0 or 2–1 up, you want to see it out. If you're drawing or you're losing, you're desperate to try to turn it around. I can't think of any situation in which I would ever feel any different if I was substituted. Of course you always put the team first, but I'm never happy at being subbed. I would worry about any player who was.

The worst one was the one I mentioned earlier for England against the USA – the first game of the 2010 World Cup. I had been ill and, looking back, I really shouldn't have played. I wasn't fit at all, I picked up a yellow card early on and I was struggling, but I was still gutted when Fabio Capello brought me off after half an hour. I knew why it was, but that didn't make it any easier, especially when it was the first game I had ever played in a World Cup.

There was one at City where Roberto Mancini substituted me and I was expecting the usual handshake as I came off, but he didn't even look at me. It was as if I wasn't there. I walked past without shaking his hand, because there was no hand to shake, and the press asked me afterwards whether there had been a bust-up. No, there hadn't, but if the manager doesn't offer his hand, what are you meant to do? I was raging as I sat on the bench. It's bad enough being substituted anyway, never mind when the manager doesn't acknowledge you.

What about coming on as a sub?

Being a sub is hard to take too. You train all week and you want to be in the starting line-up. I don't know if there are players who are happy just to be on the bench, but I've never been one of those.

Once you know you're on the bench, you've got to prepare for that. You've got to try to help the team and it's no good walking around the hotel with a face like thunder.

It's not easy to know how to warm up as a sub. You might end up coming on early, in the closing stages or not at all. You just have to make sure you're as ready – mentally and physically – as you can be. Usually the manager will send three of you out to warm up as the first half is going on. Then you'll sit down and another three will do the same and it will be rotated like that. You don't want to over-exert yourself, but some managers do it differently. Roberto Mancini only liked to send three players out to warm up because he would already have made his mind up who he was going to send on. If you weren't one of those three, you knew you weren't going to get on unless there was an injury. If you were one of the chosen three, he would send you down the touchline and you could end up warming up for 50 minutes. But what exercises can you do for 50 minutes? How many sprints down the touchline should you do? You can cover a fair bit of ground warming up non-stop for 50 minutes – and then of course, because you hadn't played, you would have your toughest session of the week the next morning.

You've got to get the warm-up right because it can be really hard to settle into a game when you're sent on. You're sitting down on the bench, then you're warming up and then you're being thrown straight into the heat of battle on 60 or 70 minutes, often with the match very delicately balanced. You've got to try to get up to pace very quickly and try to make a difference in a positive way. You're fresh, but you always feel knackered after the first few sprints. It's not easy at all to make an impact as a sub. It's like being asked to join a sprint race from a standing start.

You get some players who are very good at picking up the pace of the game straight away. I would like to think I've done that on occasion, like when Hendo and I were sent on at Southampton towards the end of last season. If you're able to give the team more energy and impetus and try to improve the performance, that's all you can do. I made a really good impact as a sub for City at Anfield when we were both going for the title in 2014. Sometimes you're able to hit the ground running and take a game by the scruff of the neck. Other times it can be really hard to adapt to the pace of the game.

What kind of instructions are you given before you come on?

For me personally, because I play quite a few positions, the first thing I need to know is where I'm coming on. Usually it's one of the three positions in midfield, but it could also be wide right, wide left, right-back, left-back. I've played up front in the past. There was a game for City at the Etihad where I played five different positions.

The manager and the coaching staff will usually give a few instructions as you're about to come on. You've probably seen players being shown things on an iPad. Those are usually just instructions for set-plays – particularly defending set-plays, where to position yourself and who to mark from corners and from various free kicks from different positions – because those things change from game to game.

That's one of the hardest things when you're coming on. If I'm coming on to do one job when defending corners or free kicks, that might mean another player has to take on a different job, so I'll also have to communicate that to him. If there's time, you do that as soon as you come on. If not, you have to make sure you do it before the next corner or free kick. It can be the difference between conceding and not.

Some managers give the substitute a note to pass to another player when they come on, mapping out any tactical changes. That's a pretty sensible way of doing it, because it should mean nothing is lost in translation, but I remember Stewart Downing once telling me that one of his managers at Boro gave him a note and the TV cameras caught him looking at it and shaking his head before screwing it up and throwing it away. I can't imagine that went down too well.

What do you have to do differently in the closing stages of a game?

If it's a close game, say if you're holding onto a one-goal lead, game management becomes so important. If you're 1–0 down and chasing the game with five minutes left, you want everything to happen as quickly as possible and you want the ball to be in play all the time with no long stoppages. If you're 1–0 up, you prefer it to be stop-start, where it's all substitutions, drawn-out free kicks and setting up for set-plays, so that it gives you a breather and takes the momentum out of the game. How many times have we seen an away team time-wasting at goal kicks when it's 0–0 and then they concede a late goal and the boot is on the other foot? At that point, the team who have been frantically hurrying around are the ones slowing things down. The roles are reversed. It's just part of the game.

Some teams are so cynical when it comes to game management that you almost have to applaud them. Italian teams, generally, are so hard to break down when they take the lead in a game. They know how to manage the game, how to break up the play, how to turn a quick free kick into a 30-second break in play. The Greek team that won the Euros in 2004 were the same. Every throw-in or free kick would be dragged out. If someone got a slight knock in midfield, they would stay down. It's frustrating as hell when you're on the wrong end of it, but it's just part of the game.

Match Day: Full Time

Are Klopp hugs as wonderful as they look? @jeremylatzke

They're wonderful when he's smiling and you know it means three points and a job well done. And then we don't really see him again until the next day. There are occasions when he'll say something in the dressing room after a game, if it's a particularly important message, but usually he prefers just to have a debrief at Melwood the next day when he's had time to watch the game again, rather than when he's hyped up and when adrenalin is running high. He will go into the room with his staff for a quick debrief and then he'll do his media duties. So those hugs that you see on the pitch are probably more important because they're the only contact we'll have with him straight after the game.

What's the post-match routine?

Obviously the mood can vary a lot, depending on the result. There will sometimes be a TV interview to do straight after the game, in the tunnel or even on the pitch, and sometimes you'll have to go straight to doping control, but the first thing you want to do is get to the dressing room. If you've picked up any kind of knock, you'll get assessed straight away.

Then we're in recovery mode, which tends to start with an ice bath. That has been part of the post-match routine for years, but it's never nice getting in, especially when it's been Baltic outside. I'll usually stay in for about six minutes. Some stay in longer. The idea is that the ice and the cold water help to reduce microtears in your muscles after exercise. We'll get our protein smoothies at the same time. After that, it's shower, get strapped up if you need to be, get changed and get some food down. As I've said before, it's vital that you get some food in your system in that first hour after the final whistle because you've got a short window after the game to try to get something inside you. That's not possible if you've got to go straight into a doping test, but the more you can take on board in that first hour, the better it is for your recovery, which is particularly important if you're playing again a few days later. I'm not a great eater and when I was younger I would often not eat at all after a game. Post-match can feel like the worst time to eat – it's the last thing I feel like doing after I've played for 90 minutes – but you learn to force it down.

After that, there'll sometimes be another round of media interviews to do. When I first started out, there would just be a few guys huddled around outside the players' entrance at Elland Road, hoping to grab us on our way to the car. These days it's totally different. We go from the dressing room into an area called the mixed zone, where there'll be loads of journalists and TV crews from all over the world, all desperate to get a quick soundbite. At Champions League matches, there are even more.

There's a certain pattern to those post-match interviews. The first two or three questions are always really gentle ones to ease you in – 'How did you think the game went?', 'You must be pleased with . . .' And then, boom, the tricky question, worded in a tricky way, where you're being asked about the opposition or the manager or the referee or something a pundit has said and you know that, unless you straight-bat it, you'll slip up. Generally I try to give safe answers. I'm asked the same questions so many times, I sometimes feel like I'm on autopilot when I answer them.

Some players really don't like doing media, particularly if it's not their first language, and they'll walk straight past the journalists, head down. There are times when I've done that too, particularly earlier in my career, but these days I don't mind doing it – unless I'm in a bad mood or I think I might say something I'd regret. It's not something I'm crazy about doing, but, as a senior player, it's part of the job. Sometimes, when you're playing every few days, with pre-match press conferences and other interviews to do, you feel like you're talking too much. There have been times when I've ended up doing so much that, if it was any other player, I'd be thinking, 'Just shut up and play football.' But someone has got to do it.

Three points, job done. What's your routine once you leave the stadium?

If it's a night match, it's straight home afterwards. If it's a weekend and you've got an evening ahead of you, then it's nice to do something socially, but it really does depend on the result. There have been many times when I've had something arranged with Amy or with friends and we've lost and I've had to cancel – or where I've gone along but I've been in a foul mood because I don't want to be out or – another thing – I don't want to be seen out, enjoying myself, if we've had a bad result.

I've tried to get better at that over the years. I used to be a lot worse for it, definitely. Hendo freely admits he's a nightmare for it. There's no way he'll go out if we've lost. I know exactly how he feels, but it's important to try to take your mind off things and not just sit at home feeling sorry for yourself. If we've got something planned, I'll try not to cancel it even if we've lost. And thankfully there haven't been too many defeats over the past couple of years at Liverpool.

If you're in a team that's struggling, it's really difficult. Newcastle weren't doing great when I was there, and the fans were frustrated. It's a massive football city, with one club, and the fans care so much. I wouldn't have wanted to show my face in the city centre after we'd lost. But you shouldn't have to put your life on hold. If it's your wife's birthday or you've arranged something with friends, then you shouldn't feel that you can't go along. I'll often just go along for the meal and then, if others are going on to a nightclub or whatever, I'll bail out at that point – because I've got training the next day anyway. I don't think anyone can criticise you for going out for a meal.

The other difficulty is when I come home from a midweek match around 11.30pm – or possibly much later. I always find it hard to sleep after games, but if it's an evening game, I can still be awake at 3am or 4am. A lot of other players will tell you the same. It's a combination of adrenalin and thinking about the game. Sometimes an incident in the game will be nagging at me and I won't be able to relax until I've watched it again. Sometimes I'll watch the whole match again, or another game that's on TV, or I'll mess about on the computer or whatever. I need to be almost dropping off by the time I go to bed. I can't lie there wide awake, trying to get to sleep. I try not to take sleeping tablets if I can, so it can be hours and hours before I drift off. And then I'm up early the next morning for training again.

Champions League Glory

How on earth did you defeat the mighty Barcelona 4–0? Was that the greatest match of your career? Please tell us about the dressing room talk. @msdevr

I would have to start by talking about the first leg at Camp Nou. We were 1–0 down, playing well, creating chances, and then Messi scored two late goals – one a wonder-goal from a free kick – to make it 3–0. That felt really harsh on the night and clearly, at that point, 3–0 down to Barcelona, not too many people were expecting us to turn it around.

We then had to go to Newcastle on the Saturday night. It was our second-to-last Premier League game and we absolutely had to win to keep the pressure on City in the title race. It was a nightmare game – really, really tough, taking the lead twice, getting pulled back twice, losing Mo to injury and then Divock (who else?) scoring a late, late winner. We had dug in and got the result we needed, but it took a heavy toll on us. Playing Wednesday, Saturday, Tuesday is always tough, particularly at that stage of the season, and it was starting to feel like everything was going against us. We had Barcelona to come on the Tuesday night, we were 3–0 down and we had lost Bobby and Mo to injury.

Then on the Monday night City were playing Leicester. Realistically, we needed them to slip up. It was looking good for us at 0–0 with 20 minutes left and then Vinny Kompany broke forward to score the goal of his life, which was like an absolute dagger to the heart. So now City were top with one game left as our thoughts turned to Barcelona. We're 3–0 down (harshly) against one of the best teams in the world, a gruelling game on the Saturday night, no Bobby, no Mo, the disappointment of the City result on the Monday night which was hard to take. It's probably fair to say we felt a bit deflated as we arrived at the training ground on the Tuesday morning.

That morning, the gaffer said to us, 'So, did everyone see that last night? Great goal, huh?' And he smiled. 'And does anyone want to talk about it?' None of us did, and I think that really took our minds off it, rather than having us stewing about it. We weren't feeling sorry for ourselves.

We were just extra motivated to beat Barcelona – or at least to give it everything we had got. I wouldn't say we went into it thinking, 'Yeah, we're definitely going to do this,' but we did have an attitude of, 'If anyone can do this, we can.' We thought, 'Let's start well, get an early goal and then we'll see what happens.'

If you can get an early goal, fantastic. But in that kind of situation, you just want to set a high tempo, do things quickly and see if you put the opposition on the back foot in the early stages. Even if it's just doing things like chasing the goalkeeper down and doing the odd crazy press just to unsettle the opposition and also get the crowd up for it. Not that our crowd needed convincing. The atmosphere was brilliant. They set the tone with the way they booed Luis Suárez as he was standing over the kick-off. I don't know if Barcelona's players knew how hostile it was going to be. That seemed to set the mood for the night.

We got a corner in the second minute, and from the roar that went up, you would have thought we had scored. After seven minutes we did score, with Divock following up Hendo's shot, and at that point Barcelona must have known we weren't just going to go out with a whimper. It was still incredibly hard, though. Messi was seeing quite a lot of the ball and, realistically, if they had scored one, it would probably have killed the tie completely. So we were defending like our lives depended on it.

Then we lost Robbo at half-time, so I had to switch to

left-back and Gini came on in midfield. But we started the second half brilliantly. Gini scored two great goals and we were back to 3–3. That was a really significant moment because when he got the third, we didn't ease off and say, 'Right, let's not lose this now. Let's hang on to what we've got.' We just went for it, full throttle, trying to get the fourth goal to kill them off. That's how it turned out.

I'm sure Barcelona's players are still livid about the fourth goal, when Trent caught them out by picking out Div with that quick corner. It's the kind of goal you would be so disappointed to concede, but at the same time, I wouldn't lay into Barcelona too much. I would prefer to give Trent credit for a great piece of quick thinking and Div for a perfect finish. Barcelona didn't produce their best performance, they know that, but they're world-class players, they've won so many trophies and they've got the player that I consider the best ever to have played the game. I think it was just the tone we set and the mentality we showed from the first minute to the last. We made it so hard for them. It was an incredible performance from us on the night. Take all those other factors into consideration – the quality of the opposition, the size of the task after the first leg, the gruelling match we played three nights earlier, the players we had missing – and it was an incredible night.

The scenes at the end were amazing. I was pretty much in tears – if not physically crying, then as close to it as you can get. It was just all the emotions of everything surrounding that game – a bit of relief, I think, as well as a lot of joy and a total sense of exhaustion after we put everything into it. Hendo was knackered and had a problem with his knee, but then he forgot at the final whistle and he did a knee slide. We were all just going mad. Then all the players and the coaching staff gathered in front of the Kop and we joined the fans in singing 'You'll Never Walk Alone'. Again, one of those moments you don't forget. But we needed to finish the job.

Was it the best feeling in the world to lift the Champions League trophy? @MajesticMilner7

Any time you win something, it's amazing. It is an incredible feeling and it can be hard to say one was better than the other because they're all special and there are different circumstances around each one.

Winning the FA Cup with Manchester City, the first trophy of the club's new era, was special. Winning the first Premier League with Manchester City a year later – and the circumstances of how we did it, with Sergio's goal in the last minute of stoppage time in the final game of the season, when it all seemed lost – was incredible. Winning it a second time in 2014, having also won the League Cup the same year, was special too. And I think everything I went through after that helped to make the Champions League win with Liverpool even more special than it already would have been.

It wasn't just my own situation, where there were people saying I had left a very successful Manchester City team and hadn't won anything at Liverpool. It was the pain we had gone through as a team over the previous few years – and the pain the fans had gone through as well. In my first season at Liverpool, we got to the League Cup final, played well and lost on penalties to City. We had that amazing night against Borussia Dortmund at Anfield in the Europa League and then we didn't finish the job in the final. We had got through to the Champions League final in 2018, with some really memorable performances and nights along the way, and then Real Madrid beat us. We had just had an unbelievable season in the Premier League, finishing with 97 points, losing only one game, and City had beaten us to it.

We didn't allow ourselves to think like this at the time, but sitting down and looking back now, I can say that there was a huge amount of pressure on us to win that final. Huge. What would it have done to the team, to the confidence, to the manager and to all of us as individuals if we had got to another final and not won it? It was my fourth final at Liverpool and we had lost the first three, so that brings an additional pressure. We were relaxed and confident beforehand, but there was a hell of a lot riding on that final. We had to finish the job.

Let's be honest about it. We didn't play well – it was probably one of our worst performances of the season – but cup finals are about winning. Nothing else. It wasn't an enjoyable game, but at that moment when Divock scored to make it 2–0 and pretty much settled things with a couple of minutes left, well, you can see how much it meant to us all. I've watched it back and Alisson fell onto his knees and Virg was flat on his back. The rest of us were all celebrating with Div. If I was trying to describe the feeling, I would call it a surge of joy and relief. It's the best feeling you can have. Celebrating with your team-mates and the fans and knowing you're very nearly there. The atmosphere had been tense all evening, but from that moment, it was like a party was going on in the stands. It was brilliant.

From that surge, there was a need to come down quickly because there were a few minutes left to play. We had to finish off. Ali still had to make a couple of saves after that, but the last couple of minutes, there was a strong feeling among the lads of, 'Come on. We've got this.'

How did you feel at the final whistle? Sean Barrett

Again, it was players falling to their knees, punching the air, pointing to the skies. There were man-hugs everywhere. All the subs were running on to join the celebrations and we were all just grabbing whoever was closest. Hendo was in tears and I wasn't far off. It was just a feeling of, 'We've done it. After all that we've been through, we've done it.'

Very quickly, though, almost immediately, you remember that there's another side to it because all the Spurs players looked distraught. We went over to commiserate with them. There's not really much you can say apart from 'Sorry, unlucky,' but we knew how they were feeling, having been through it in Kiev the previous year.

And after that, I looked around and we were all at the Spurs end of the stadium, next to the goal we had been defending in the second half, and all our fans were at the other end, so I thought, 'Sod this' and marched over to our fans and gave it the six fingers. We had won it together, with their help, and I knew how much the sixth European Cup meant to them. That went down well. Then I saw Matt, our press officer, who was crying his eyes out, so I went over and celebrated with him. Then all the rest of the boys ran down and started celebrating in front of our fans.

I don't know how long we were out there celebrating before the trophy presentation. At that moment you're just on a massive high. You're thinking of everything you've done to get there, of what you've been through together as a team, of what the fans have been through, particularly the ones who have travelled all over Europe to watch us, and – a big one this – you're thinking about how much it means to your family. It means so much to have them supporting you. You don't want them to come all that way and see you lose another final. Winning it was for them.

Did you really decline an invitation from Jordan Henderson to lift the trophy?

Kind of. Just before the presentation, we lined up to give Spurs' players a guard of honour. That was all thanks to Hendo. I had completely forgotten, so fair play to him for that because I know we appreciated it when Real Madrid did the same for us in Kiev the year before.

After the Spurs players had gone past, Hendo shouted, 'Milly.' 'What?' 'Let's lift it together.' 'What?' 'The trophy. You and me. Let's lift it together.' I gave him my usual face. Was he winding me up? Absolutely no chance. I said to him, 'Hendo, if anyone other than you lifts that trophy, they're getting wrestled to the ground. This is all you.'

In Hendo's mind, it's never about him. It's always about the team. But it was his moment, whether he liked it or not. He had been at the club for eight years, taking some unfair stick at times, and he had joined that great list of captains who had led Liverpool to victory in the European Cup final – Emlyn Hughes, Phil Thompson, Graeme Souness, Steven Gerrard and now Jordan Henderson. He had earned the right. It shows the kind of guy he is that he wanted to share the moment, but I wouldn't have wanted to get in the way. And looking at his face as he lifted the trophy, I would say he quite enjoyed it in the end. I've no idea how he managed to find the energy to do his fast-feet routine, but maybe that's what winning the European Cup does for you.

It was a great moment for all of us. I haven't got a clue how many of the other lads lifted the trophy before I did. It didn't bother me whether I was second or 22nd. Seeing all my mates lift that trophy – what a moment. We've all been on different journeys in our careers and we've all had big disappointments to get over at various times, including in Kiev 12 months earlier.

Out of everyone, Hendo was probably the one I was happiest for. He's an amazing person and an amazing captain who always put everyone else ahead of himself. The team always comes first with Hendo. That won't change, but I do think maybe this success will help him realise what a brilliant player he is.

What were the celebrations like in the dressing room and on the parade next day? Oliver King

I don't know how long we were on the pitch for afterwards. We spent ages dancing around the trophy and lifting it up in front of the fans, again singing along with them to 'You'll Never Walk Alone'. Then we managed to get the families down onto the pitch to join us, which was special for all of us. Standing on the pitch with Amy and my sister Claire, with the European Cup at our feet, with our kids running around and picking up the confetti, was one of those moments I'll always treasure.

We finally went back to the dressing room and everyone

was buzzing. There are a few videos of us singing and shouting and messing around. Then it was time for a few post-match interviews – the easiest ones any of us will ever do. Eventually we all got onto the bus, with Ali bringing on the trophy to a massive cheer. All the way back to the hotel, we were all on a massive high, banging on the windows and the ceiling of the bus, and every single one of us joined in as we belted out 'Sweet Caroline'. The party back at our hotel was great. Amy and Claire couldn't stay long because they were flying back early the next morning, but it was really nice to have them there. There were loads of people there – not just the players but their families and all the staff, including the people who do the unseen work at Melwood day in, day out – and the really good thing was that everyone there had contributed to it. The younger players were there too and I can only imagine how that must feel. You would just think, 'This is it. I want to be part of this.'

Everyone was on a high. It got quite loud and a bit messy, as you would expect. Some of the lads had the microphone and were singing. I can't remember what time I went to bed, but I had about two hours' sleep. A lot of the lads had less. None at all in some cases. The party didn't really end. One of the security guys brought the trophy upstairs when we were having breakfast, so Ads and I said, 'That's going on our table.' Brekkie with the European Cup – I can recommend it.

The flight home was quite chilled out. We had some tunes

on and some of the lads tried to catch up on some sleep. We all felt tired at the start of the parade, but just seeing the crowds of people gave us another energy boost. I was right at the front of the bus with Robbo, in the corner, and we started getting some chants going – 'Allez, allez, allez' and all that – and just enjoying it with the fans. It was good to see there were a few Everton fans there as well, knocking about in blue shirts in the middle of it all. Most of them were giving it some good banter. One bloke in a window gave us some not-such-good banter, so I got the cup and waved it at him.

The parade is something I'll never forget. All of it was good, but the last bit, as we reached the city centre, was incredible with the number of fans and the noise and just a sea of red. As a group of players, we had come from all over the world – South America, North Africa, West Africa, all over Europe and all over Britain. Trent was the only local lad in the 23-man squad for the final, but I think every single one of us felt that the parade was something incredibly special. It was one of those moments you live for as a footballer. Ali was bawling his eyes out, he felt so emotional, and I can understand why, seeing how much our victory meant to the fans. Then you see the videos of what it meant to other fans all over the world and to your own family and friends, who send you messages and pictures and videos of them celebrating it, and you're left with this incredibly warm feeling that you hope will last for ever.

We had another party back at Anfield afterwards, which was the first time I'd seen my parents since the match. I thought of everything they had done for me over the years and I remembered how disappointed I felt for them after we lost in the final the year before. They had travelled all the way to Kiev to support me and I felt like I had let them down, so it was great to see them and my uncle and auntie, who also go to most games, looking so happy and so proud. I felt as happy for them as I did for myself.

I just wish we had had another three or four days to celebrate it together, but then most of the lads went off on international duty and we went on holiday. As I've said before, there really isn't all that much time to bask in the glory of it all before your thoughts turn to the new season and trying to do it all over again.

How many bottles of Ribena does it take to fill up the European Cup? @jell_1982

Haven't I said how much I resent questions like this?

Okay, I'll be honest. I've been thinking about this a lot. A lot.

Using my GCSE maths (grade A), I decided to measure it. UEFA's website says the trophy is 73.5 cm tall, but the dimensions are all over the place. I don't know who designed it. It's a circle at the top, but then it widens before curving down and tapering almost to a point at the bottom. So this wasn't going to be easy. Rather than estimate, I decided I was going to work it out in cross-sections at 1 cm intervals.

And then it became clear that was going to take for ever, so instead I got a load of 2 litre bottles of water and poured them into it. It turns out the European Cup can hold *precisely* 36 litres of water. Who knew?

But that isn't the end of the matter. You specifically asked 'how many bottles of Ribena'. Well, I've debated this with some of my team-mates and we're pretty unanimous that 'Ribena' refers to the undiluted cordial, as sold, rather than the diluted version. And by 'bottles', I'm referring to the standard 500 ml bottles rather than the bigger varieties. If I poured 36 litres of undiluted Ribena into the European Cup, it would seriously tarnish the silver. Trust me – you don't want to go there. And that's before we talk about the damage to your teeth. So I'm going to have to dilute it. Then it becomes a question of taste. The manufacturers suggest that you work to a ratio of one part cordial to four parts water, but I find it's still a little bit too sweet like that. So I like to work to a ratio of two parts cordial to seven parts water. (If you find the ratio difficult to work with, just pre-mix 900 ml and drink it throughout the week.)

Based on that ratio, to fill the European Cup, I would need 8 litres of Ribena cordial and 28 litres of water. That means 16 bottles of undiluted cordial. Armed with that knowledge, you're probably better off buying ten of the 850 ml bottles

– slightly better value that way – and you'll have half a litre left over for later.

Another little tip: if you're drinking it from the most prestigious trophy in club football, you might be better off pouring the water in first and the cordial on top. Then give it a good mix. At that point, I would need to drink it fairly quickly, so I would need some of my team-mates to help me out. And Robbo prefers Irn-Bru, so it's all a bit of a quandary. Anyway, there's your answer. Drink responsibly. Other blackcurrant cordials are available.

Words of Advice

Would you encourage your son or daughter to play football?
Hettie Smith

I would always encourage them to try every sport and to do it to be healthy and to enjoy themselves. It's important to learn about being part of a team, too. It helps you think of others and to develop team spirit rather than just thinking about yourself.

Our children are already working out what they like. They both love swimming. My daughter is a proper little princess who loves everything girly and my boy loves running around and throwing himself about like a nutter. He's really starting to get into his football. If he was to be talented enough and lucky enough to get into a professional football academy, would I encourage him? I would just encourage him to do what he's happy doing. I wouldn't pressure him to.

As a parent, you just want your kids to be happy. It's fantastic that there are great rewards in professional football, but there are also certain pitfalls and things you wouldn't want them to have to face. That's life, though. There are ups and downs in anything you do. I just want them to do what they're happy doing.

I play for my school team and for a local under-11s team and would love to play professionally when I'm older. What is the best advice to try to get scouted? Danny-Lee Mitchell-Brunt

It's so hard. You've got to work hard on your game, play well, be lucky and, if you're good enough, word will usually get around. Everton spotted me when I was playing for my district team in Crosby. Then Leeds saw me playing for another team. There's a bit of luck involved, but ultimately if you're playing well enough on a consistent basis, your name is going to get about. There are plenty of scouts out there watching youth football.

I don't think anyone should obsess about trying to be scouted. Just play your own game. Play to your strengths and do the best job possible for your team. If there's a scout there or if you're on trial – or in fact, just a general piece of advice – don't do anything purely to try to stand out. People love watching tricks and stepovers and fancy crosses on YouTube, and of course it looks great, but in a team sport, it's about output and winning games. Ultimately, if you're doing 15 stepovers but your crossing is poor, you're not going to impress anyone. You're far more likely to catch the eye if you're able to receive the ball smoothly, get it out of your feet, create a yard of space and put a great ball over to set up a chance for a team-mate. But above all, at that age, just try to enjoy your football.

Were you ever told you were too small to play for an academy team? What would you tell a nine-year-old who was overlooked because of his size, not his actual ability? @DickensonDiane

No one ever told me I was too small, but I had a friend at Leeds who was released for that reason. Then, funnily enough, he grew about four inches in the next 18 months after that, but he wasn't invited back, which was a shame.

There was another player in the academy who was one of the best technical players I had ever seen at that age – unbelievable, he was – but he was tiny and he never got a sniff and ended up getting released. When I was with England under-15s and under-16s, it often felt like they just picked the biggest guys. I was on the bench at first. If you were already pushing six feet at that age and you could play a bit too, you got in the team.

A lot of people have said that English football put too

much emphasis on height and strength in those days, which means that at youth level they sometimes picked players who were like men at 16, rather than picking those who might have been more skilful but hadn't finished growing. That seems to have changed a lot now, with more emphasis on technique, but I'm sure there are still times when talented young players lose out simply because of their height.

I just think, well, look at Lionel Messi. If you're good enough, it doesn't matter how big or small you are. If you're not big, you need to think how you might combat that and how you might compensate in other areas. If you've got a low centre of gravity, that can be a real advantage because you can twist and turn quicker than other players. You can use that in your favour, but you need to be strong and learn how to use your body well. If you do that, it can be hard for people to knock you off the ball.

Look at Andy Robertson, too. He was released by Celtic for being 'too small' when he was 15 and look at him now. He's about average height now anyway, but you can tell he has worked so hard on his game – as well as filling out by eating plenty of shortbread. I don't think anyone would even give his height a second thought now.

It's important to work hard on your technique, particularly your receiving skills and that ability to twist and turn in tight spaces. That's true of any player, no matter what your size, but particularly so for smaller players so that you get into space and into the right position and use your body so that you're not going straight into a 50/50 challenge. If your receiving skills are good and you know how to use a low centre of gravity to your advantage, then your height won't be such an issue. You're unlikely to win many headers if you're small, but there are still ways of doing it if you position yourself right and time your jump well. Giving your opponent a little nudge won't do any harm either. If you're clever and learn how to use your body, you can make being small work to your advantage. More and more coaches these days see it that way too. But if you're nine years old, it's safe to say you've got plenty of time to grow.

I have always thought my best position is central midfield, but this season my coach has been playing me at centre-back. What advice would you give to a young player who feels frustrated by having to play in a different position he doesn't enjoy? Cosmo Kay

I know exactly how you're feeling because I've played in a lot of positions in my career and it can be frustrating when you're not playing in the one that you feel is your best.

It depends on the reasons. Are you being asked to play there just to fill in because there's no one else? Or are you playing there because your coach feels that it suits your skillset? There are so many players at the highest level who started out in midfield and ended up as central defenders. A lot of full-backs started out as wingers. People tend not to like it at first when they're asked to play an unfamiliar position, but often they adapt, do well and it works out really well for their career. Look at someone like Trent at Liverpool. He was always a midfielder until one of the academy coaches suggested he would make a top-class full-back – and the coach was 100 per cent right. Trent is a fantastic lad with a great attitude. He took everything on board – and look at him now. If anything, you might be getting a head-start on other players by playing in defence.

For a team to function properly, you need players doing all different jobs, pulling in the same direction. You've got a choice to make. If you want to speak to your coach about it, make sure you do that in the right way rather than kicking up a fuss. Don't go chucking your toys out of the pram or go onto the pitch with the wrong attitude. If you can understand your coach's reasons for wanting to play you in a different position, that should help. I'll always say it's more important for boys and girls to enjoy their football than anything else, but as it becomes more competitive as you get older, there are times when you might have to adapt your game and make compromises for the good of the team. And although it might not feel that way at the time, that can bring real benefits to your development as a player too. The team always comes first, but think of the possibilities for you as a player rather than just the downsides. Playing in different positions can help you become a better player with a deeper understanding of the game.

This year my team will make the jump to 11-a-side pitches and bigger balls and goals. Do you have any tips on how we can make the transition? Josh Butler

I'm assuming you're moving into under-13 football, in which case you're lucky because the first game I ever played was on a full-size pitch with full-size goals, which was just ridiculous when I was eight. When I started playing at the academy at Leeds, we used smaller pitches and I think we moved on to full-size pitches when we were in the under-14s. It's a big jump in terms of the size of the pitches and obviously your fitness levels need to be much higher, because you're having to run so much further, but hopefully that comes as you're growing. It's more demanding physically, but you might find it easier in terms of finding space and time on the ball. The spaces are different. There are pluses and minuses. If you're a forward, you'll find that there's more space to exploit – and if you semi-shank a shot, it still might go in because the goals are bigger. If you're a defender, it could be harder at first because you're defending a big space. That will take some getting used to.

As a player who is admired for his work ethic, do you agree with the theory that anyone can master any skill if they work hard enough at it? James Taylor

I certainly believe in hard work, in whatever you do, but I think the theory you're talking about is that if you spend 10,000 hours practising something, you can become an expert. I'm not sure I believe that. I could practise basketball for 10,000 hours but I wouldn't make it as a NBA player because I'm not tall enough and I don't have the physique for it. I would always encourage anyone to work as hard as possible to try to get better at something you enjoy doing. But I'm not sure you can apply that 10,000-hour 'rule' to football either. You could be incredibly dedicated and practise football non-stop, which would improve your technique beyond all recognition, but what about the physical aspect and the tactical aspect and understanding the game? I think people underestimate just how important hard work and dedication is, but equally people can underestimate the basic skillset that you need in terms of physical and technical attributes and the understanding of the game. You don't just need one or two parts of that package. You need all of it.

I would love to be able to tell people that if they practise enough, they will make it to the Premier League. I wish it was as straightforward as that. But practising as much as you can certainly won't do you any harm. It will give you the best chance of being as good as you can be.

What advice would you give to young girls who have a passion for football? @MagicMo11LFC

Exactly the same advice that I would give to boys: play football – or any sport – to enjoy it. If you get to the stage where it's becoming more competitive and more serious, and if you keep enjoying it, that's great.

There are so many more opportunities now for girls and women to play football. When I started out, you really didn't hear much about women's football. It didn't even get much attention within the clubs. These days, all the leading clubs have women's teams and a lot of the players have gone professional. There has been a lot of investment in the women's game in England – not just at professional level but at grass-roots, with girls encouraged to play from a young age – and we've seen the benefits of that with the national team reaching the past two World Cup semi-finals.

I know Steph Houghton well. We have the same agent and she joined Manchester City while I was there. She's a great player and a brilliant role model with the way she approaches the game, all the work she has done as an ambassador for football and everything she does away from the pitch. I've got so much admiration for her.

It has been great to see the England team doing so well. I didn't see all of the World Cup, but I watched a number of the games and was impressed by the way they played. Appointing Phil Neville as coach was a good move because you can see how committed to it he is. I'm sure his profile, with everything he has done in men's football, has been positive for the profile of women's football too.

One thing that has happened in recent years is that there has been a lot more integration between the men's and women's teams. I first became aware of that at City, where the women's team shared the training ground when the club moved to the Etihad Campus. A lot of the staff worked across both teams, whereas in the past the women's team wouldn't have had access to the same resources. At Liverpool the women's team joined us on our pre-season tour of America. We all played games in South Bend, Boston and New York. The club has a slogan that says 'two teams but one club'. That's exactly right. Women's football has made huge progress in this country over the past ten years. The way things are going, it's only going to grow and grow, which is great.

James, I was an awesome footballer. I had almost everything – bar mental strength, which meant I was never going to make it. It took till I was 28 and playing in Oz to realise that. Can you tell when a youth doesn't have the mentality to make it? And is it coached? @FourTwoThreeOne

I'd say the mental side of it, as opposed to pure technical ability, is a much bigger factor than most people realise. If you were going to put it in percentage terms of what's needed in order to have a good career, I would say mentality is at least 50 per cent of it. First, there's knowing what you're doing in a game. Second, there's having the inner drive to stay focused and keep striving to get the best out of your ability.

Beyond that, if you can get yourself into a place where you're playing regular football at a good level, there's the question of whether you are mentally strong enough to sustain that over the course of a career. And that doesn't just mean staying at the level you are, which is hard enough. It means you have to keep striving to get better, while dealing with all the things that come up from one week to the next: injuries, loss of form, not being in the team, criticism from fans or the media, playing in hostile atmospheres and so on. Different people react in different ways. If you have a bad game or you get sent off or criticised, whether it's by your manager or the fans or the media, then you need to learn to handle that kind of adversity.

And it's not just dealing with the lows but also with the highs. You see players who achieve some kind of break-through – training with the first team, making their debut, getting a new contract, breaking into the England squad, winning a trophy – and, instead of kicking on from that, some of them ease off.

It's hard to say whether that mentality is something you're born with or whether it's something you can develop, but you can often recognise with a young player of 18 or 19 whether he's got the right mentality or not. If he has, you encourage him to keep going. If not, you try to steer him in the right direction.

A lot of it has to come from the standards that are drummed into you when you're young, whether that's by parents, coaches or whatever. There are ways of improving on that side of things when you're older, though. Psychologists can be a big help. Being a quick learner – and a willing learner – is extremely important too. It's okay making mistakes, which everyone does at some point, but the ones who go on to have good careers are the ones who learn from those mistakes. A really strong, professional team environment will help that. Maybe in the wrong kind of dressing room, a player can pick up bad habits. In the right kind of dressing room, with the right type of manager and senior players around him, he will be encouraged to learn from mistakes rather than being allowed to repeat them again and again. By setting the right example, senior players can have an important part to play in the way young players develop. If a young player is willing to take in information from the players and coaches around him, that's invaluable. It's important for any team to have good senior players. I learned a lot from watching guys like Gary Speed, Aaron Hughes and Alan Shearer at Newcastle. Sometimes just watching the way they go about their business, on and off the pitch, can really benefit a young player.

There are examples where the penny drops for players a

bit later in their careers and they develop a mentality that perhaps wasn't there when they were younger. If you've dropped down to non-league level, like Jamie Vardy, then getting back to the top takes a huge amount of mental strength. Jamie says himself that he didn't really have that belief when he was 16 or 17; he had the drive, but not the focus. But he has become the perfect example of someone who developed the mentality and the attitude that has helped him get back to the top and have a career that was probably beyond anything he dreamed of when he was younger. I've got so much respect for the way Jamie and other players have done that. That shows that the right mentality can be developed later in a career, but it's not the norm.

What advice would you give young players who are just starting their journey in the game? @oliver_golden1

If you mean when they're at a very young age, playing at amateur level, I would just encourage them to enjoy it. If you mean further down the line, when they've signed for a club, whether that's with an academy or signing full-time at 16, then my advice would be all about working as hard as possible and trying to make the most of the opportunity that is in front of them.

Over the years I've seen players who have had so much ability but haven't had the right attitude. They've blown it and thrown it away, almost before realising the opportunity they had. Then there have been other players who haven't had anything like as much ability, but their attitude has helped get them to the top. Then there are the guys who have incredible ability and a great attitude – and they're world-beaters.

Seeing wasted talent does frustrate me. I'm not talking about players who get injured. I'm talking about the ones who have amazing ability but don't seem willing to work hard to make the most of it. When you've been around a bit, at different clubs over a number of years, you know what's going to happen to the vast majority of players who are like that. Even if they get to the top, they might stay there for a few months, or a year or two at the most, but they'll just fall away again unless they develop the right mentality.

So my advice would be: listen to your coaches and team-mates; be honest with yourself about what you need to improve; train hard and work on your weaknesses; don't be afraid to ask questions or to take responsibility for your career; and don't just be a sheep and follow everyone else.

The harsh reality of football is that most players don't get anywhere near the top, even if they're incredibly talented in their early teens. The odds are stacked overwhelmingly against you, especially these days, when the opportunities for homegrown players are so limited. The ones who have the right attitude are aware of the task ahead of them and make sure they do everything possible to give themselves the best chance of making it at the highest level they can. But over the years I've seen other lads who, as soon as they sign for a club, think they've made it. I can understand how that happens. They're training in amazing facilities from seven years old, they've got all the pristine training kit, they get boots given to them, they play on beautiful pitches and, while they might feel that they train hard, they've never really had to graft for any of it. They don't have to clean boots and do odd jobs to keep their feet on the ground like we did when we were apprentices at Leeds. It's totally different now.

There are various points where a player, even if he doesn't have the right attitude, might feel that he's 'made it'. That could happen at a young age, when he first starts training with a big club at an academy, or when he starts a scholarship at 16 or when he gets his first professional contract or when he starts training with the first team or makes his debut or gets an England call-up or anything like that. I've seen so many players at different clubs get to various points and then ease off – and you can't help thinking that it's because, subconsciously, they've allowed themselves to think that they've made it.

I used to see certain young players and think to myself, 'Do you realise the opportunity that is in front of you? And do you realise how hard you're going to have to work to make the most of that opportunity? You've taken your foot off the gas and if you carry on the way you're going, you'll drop down the leagues and it will be over in a few years. Just give it everything you've got.'

As an experienced player, you've got a responsibility to give the players the right type of encouragement and advice. You've got to be constructive, but at the same time you need to make them aware of the challenges, the pitfalls and the need to give it everything.

You hear it all the time. 'Such-and-such was as good as Wayne Rooney when he was 17.' But talent is only one part of the equation. I look back to the England teams I played in at youth level: there were players who I was certain would make it to the very top – 100 per cent – who just fell away. Sometimes it's injuries, sometimes it's luck, circumstances, opportunities or whatever. And when that happens, I always sympathise with the player. But when it's because someone thinks he has made it at 17 or because he's focusing too much on the wrong things – enjoying himself too much or wasting money on stuff that he really shouldn't even be thinking about at that age – it's extremely frustrating to see. As a senior player, you can keep telling players that, but ultimately they have to take responsibility for their own careers.

The Future

Name one player you would like Liverpool to sign.
@LiverPaul8

I've probably paid Lionel Messi enough compliments already in this book, and I really don't think he'll ever leave Barcelona, so I'll say Kylian Mbappé. Such an exciting player with years ahead of him. We're not exactly short of top-class goalscorers, though.

Last season you made your 500th Premier League appearance. You're now fifth in the all-time Premier League list. Ahead of you are Gary Speed, David James, Frank Lampard, Ryan Giggs and your old mate Gareth Barry, who made 653. Would you ever be motivated by trying to break that record?

I would never make career decisions based on trying to break it, but it definitely felt nice to join the 500 club – especially because we had a good win that day at Bournemouth. Rio Ferdinand texted me to say 'Welcome to the club.' That was nice of him.

I played with all of those players except Ryan Giggs. I also played with Emile Heskey, Steven Gerrard and Jamie Carragher, who all played 500-plus, so maybe I've learned a few good habits from them over the years.

Hopefully in this book I've given some sense of the kind of commitment you need in order to have a long, successful career at the highest level. It's why I take my hat off to someone like Ryan Giggs, for having the drive to keep playing as long as he did, beyond his 40th birthday, and keep wanting to win things year after year. Gareth Barry doesn't get the same recognition, but he is like a machine and he's still going in the Championship with West Brom. He is such an under-rated player in English football. He has been so consistent everywhere he has played, including for the national team, and was a huge part in our successes at Manchester City.

I've been around a long time too and I've looked after myself. I've been lucky enough to play for five great clubs in the Premier League (and I don't forget the six appearances I made on loan to Swindon either). To have any kind of career in football takes some doing. It's not something I spend much time thinking about, but to play 500-plus games in the Premier League, for the clubs I have, is definitely something I can be proud of. I'm sure it's something I'll look back on at the end of my career. I would like to think I've got a good few years left – touch wood – but I'm not even going to think about breaking Gaz's record. That's still some way off and I would never want to look too far ahead.

You've literally won everything. Would you like to finish your career at Leeds United? A poetic bookend to a marvellous and ridiculously under-rated/under-appreciated career? @ChrisNLangley

I get asked this all the time. Any time I bump into a Leeds fan – or even my mates back home – it's always, 'When are you coming back? When are you coming home?'

It's a really hard question to answer because it's all totally hypothetical. There has never been a decision for me to make. They've never come in for me in the past and they might not do so in future. I'm playing for a great team who have just won the Champions League. Am I happy at Liverpool? Absolutely.

About Leeds, all I can really say is that I still love the club and I still love the fans. It's a regret that I didn't play for Leeds longer. I didn't want to leave and I felt like I was only really getting started at the club, but it was an unfortunate time for me to be coming through at Leeds. They had been in the Champions League semi-final in 2001, but by the time I made my debut 18 months later, a lot of players had been sold and the club was going into a decline. I'll never forget how brilliant the fans were with us the day we were relegated in 2004, after what was a pretty horrible couple of years for Leeds, and they've been fantastic throughout the 15 years since, standing by the team through thick and thin. When I see the atmosphere at Elland Road and I hear the crowd, it makes me proud. The fan relationship changes when you're a professional player and you move on to different clubs, but I still follow them and look out for their scores every weekend. Watching *Take Us Home*, you get a real feeling for how desperate everyone is for the club to get back to the Premier League, where it belongs.

To go back and play for my hometown club again would be amazing in so many different ways. But at the same time, they say 'Never go back,' don't they? What happens if you go back and it isn't the fairy-tale finish? Would it be the right thing for me? Would it be the right thing for them? There would be so many things to weigh up – not just for myself or my family but for Leeds. If I was being released by another club, would they want me? It would be pointless for them and for me if I wasn't needed at the time and it was just some kind of nostalgia trip. You can probably tell from what I'm saying that I love the club, but I also love playing for Liverpool and I want to play at the highest level for as long as I can. If my time at Liverpool came to an end and I was going to go somewhere else and Leeds were one of the clubs that were interested in me, then that would be a very exciting option for all the reasons I mention. But they might not be interested. I might look abroad. Something else could crop up that I've never even thought of. It is a nice idea, but I can't say what the future will hold.

You've only ever played for English teams, and even though the outside world is very much in the EPL, you never gave a European club a chance. How come? Were/are there no offers out there? I can't imagine that being the case! @Keay_163

My agent Matthew would be able to tell you more, but when I was in the final six months of my contract at City, which meant I could have signed a pre-contract agreement with an overseas club, there was serious interest from some big clubs in Italy and Spain. Four to five of them got in touch with Matthew – really good clubs – but it never got as far as me sitting down with any of them. I would have been entitled to do that because I was in the final six months, but out of respect for City, because I was still negotiating with them at the time, I just wanted to focus on playing.

The only club I spoke to was Liverpool and that was when the season was over.

Liverpool was the option that really appealed to me, but going to play in Spain or Italy would definitely have had its charms. Everything about it is appealing – not just the sunshine. It would be nice to experience a different lifestyle and a different league. I think the style of football would appeal to me too. I can speak Spanish, so the idea of a language barrier wouldn't have concerned me at all.

I don't know what the future holds. I definitely would consider going abroad in future, depending how long I carry on playing. Whether that meant playing in Europe or going to MLS or wherever, I think it would be a great experience both on and off the pitch, but I'm in no rush to leave Liverpool and, on top of that, it's very important that you consider the impact on your family, especially when you've got young children. It might be a great move for your family, but you would have to weigh everything up. It's not just your own life or situation that you have to think about. It's about what's best for your family.

Would you consider moving to Rangers or Celtic? Scotland?
@jackpaton20

It's not something I've ever thought about before, simply because it has never come up. Again it's all hypothetical, but they are two massive clubs with great support. They're the kind of clubs that players love playing for. We did a charity game up at Celtic, for Stan Petrov and for my foundation, and the crowd were brilliant. It was so well supported. Robbo never stops talking about Celtic and I know Steven Gerrard has been really struck by the size of Rangers since he went there. They're both huge clubs. I wouldn't like to give an opinion about which is bigger . . .

Why haven't the players backed the @savegrassroots campaigns? @AintreeAjax

I'm not aware of the campaign that you mention, but if it's about investing in grass-roots sports facilities, I'm all in favour of that. One of the things my foundation has been helping with is community sports facilities in deprived areas. Everything starts at grass-roots level and it's a big problem when you see so many pitches being sold for housing. It's important that there are enough pitches – and that the pitches are looked after, not covered with glass and dog muck. It needs to be a safe, clean environment for kids to play in. Grass-roots is where everything starts, whether it's at school or in a local team, so it's vital that there are facilities there for people to play.

Have you achieved all you wanted as a footballer? Or is there more to come from James Milner, maybe coaching? And if so, which club would be your no. 1 to coach? @PeterWDoyle

I definitely want to achieve more as a player. I want to win more trophies with Liverpool. If I move on somewhere else after Liverpool, I'll want to achieve things there.

I don't know about coaching and management yet. Sometimes I think it would be great. Other times I'm less sure. On one hand, it would feel like a waste if I didn't, considering everything I've learned and everyone I've worked with, from Terry Venables to Jürgen Klopp. I do feel like I would potentially have something to offer, and it would be interesting, but then you look at the amount of work involved in order to get to UEFA Pro Licence level. I have done as far as Level Two, but then it would be B Licence, A Licence, Pro Licence and that takes years. I could try to work on my B Licence now, but I'm playing for a club where I'll be expected to play 50-odd games a season at the highest level, and I've got a young family, plus various other interests, such as my foundation, and I can't really see where I would fit it in. I don't know how long I'll carry on playing, but if, hypothetically, I played for another three seasons after this one, that would take me to 37. If I do my B Licence then, how long would it take to get to Pro Licence level? Obviously I recognise the need to educate coaches and bring them to certain standards, but I think a lot of players end up being put off by how long and painstaking the whole process is, particularly those who have had long careers at top level.

I like the idea of coaching or managing. I've enjoyed it when I've done it. It's interesting watching things unfold, within a match or a session, and making different observations and points. These days you see some players go into other jobs, like director of football. That's interesting too, running the club, forward planning, making sure things are right. But if you're going straight into a job as a coach or a manager or that type of role, it's full-on, exactly the same kind of life again, very pressurised, and you have to weigh up whether that's the right thing for you and your family. After 20-odd years on the treadmill, is that what I would want? Maybe I would prefer to take a break and work out what I wanted to do, rather than rush into anything.

I have a few other business interests and, of course, the foundation. There are a few things that appeal to me and it would probably be a case of slowly working out what I wanted to do. You could try coaching or TV or something else and love it. Equally you could hate it. You might desperately miss the day-to-day involvement of being in a dressing room. I think I'll probably wait until I'm a year or two from retiring before I start to think seriously about the next step. And I'm not at that stage yet. There are still a lot of challenges left for me as a footballer.

If you retired tomorrow, how do you think you would do if you played Sunday League? Andy Welsh

To be clear on this one, Welshy has been one of my best mates since we were young and this is something we've debated over the years. He was a good player when we were kids – good dribbler, great left foot – and he went on to play for Horsforth Dynamos, but I wasn't allowed to play junior football or for the school team or anything once I signed for Leeds' academy, so we never actually played together.

If you had asked me this 15 years ago when I was a winger and a bit more of a dribbler, I would probably have thought I would have torn it up and scored loads of goals. But these days I'm a bit more of a passer and I need the likes of Mo and Sadio to get on the end of things. And with the greatest respect to you, Welshy, you've put a bit of timber on over the past ten years, so I'm not sure you would be able to play that role in the same way that Mo does.

One slightly sad thing about being a professional footballer is that I've never even been able to have a proper kickaround with my mates. I've heard of other players doing it, playing five-a-side or whatever, but I just wouldn't risk it. What if I got injured?

I'm sure it would be enjoyable. It would be completely different. As someone who is lucky enough to play with some great footballers week in and week out, it would probably also be frustrating as hell at times.

When you're playing for Liverpool, you don't just pass the ball to your team-mate. You're always having to think two passes ahead. You know whether to pass it to someone's right foot or their left foot. You know whether you're going to zing it into them because they want to knock it around the corner for someone else. If I was playing with a Sunday League team, then no disrespect, that would probably have to go out of the window. I could zing it to a team-mate to knock it first time because I know where his next pass should be. But he might not know that himself. I'm sure it would be frustrating. Fun, but frustrating.

The flip-side of this question would be the one about how a Sunday League player would do if he was dropped into the Liverpool team for a Premier League game. I do think Welshy would be able to play a few decent passes if he could get any kind of time on the ball – he was always a good technical player – but what would shock any player is how fast and physically demanding Premier League games are. I'm sure most Sunday League players would be blowing out of their backside within five minutes. I wouldn't worry about Welshy receiving the ball in tight spaces, but then again I'm remembering him from 15 years ago. He's more of a rounded player now.

You do get some very talented players at Sunday League level, though. Some of them – with different circumstances, a lucky break here or there – could easily have had a professional career. I think amateur players can probably underestimate how hard it is to perform at the highest level, but equally I'm sure a lot of professional players would find Sunday League hard in certain ways. You might play lots of great passes, but if there's no one on the same wavelength, or no one with the speed to get on to them, then that would be frustrating. Depending on the type of player you are, it must be incredibly difficult to be really technical on awful pitches, playing with players who aren't at the same standard as yourself. And then there's the extra challenge of doing all of that when you've had ten pints and a curry the night before. I take my hat off to people who can do that.

What is the proudest moment of your career? @Tomasu90

I'm proud of my whole career, playing for great clubs, winning trophies, playing for my country. I know I've been incredibly lucky, but I also know I have worked extremely hard for everything I've done.

Not everything about being a professional footballer is as picture-perfect as it might appear from the outside, but I've always appreciated how lucky I am. You have to know that you need to make sacrifices. Things don't just fall into your lap. Or if that does happen for some players, that won't be the case for long if you're not prepared to work and make sacrifices.

Football has given me so much, on and off the pitch, but I'm also proud that the career I've had has given me an opportunity to be able to help people. I'm fortunate enough to be in a position to be able to do that, so I set up the JM7 Foundation to try to give something back. It was initially going to be about trying to raise money for the NSPCC, which I've been an ambassador for since I was 18, and Help For Heroes, which is the charity we supported with England, as well as trying to develop sports facilities for young people, particularly in under-privileged areas in the cities where I've played. We've raised money for the Leeds Rhinos foundation, for a netball team in Manchester who needed new facilities, for kids in Liverpool so that they had opportunities to go on football camps in the school holidays.

Just before we were about to launch the foundation in 2012, my old Villa team-mate Stan Petrov, a great player and a really great guy, was diagnosed with leukaemia, so we added Bloodwise to the list of charities we were supporting. Stan now has the Stiliyan Petrov Foundation. We worked together to set up the 'Match for Cancer' between Celtic and Liverpool legends at Celtic Park in 2018. That raised money for both of our foundations, plus Celtic's foundation. Most recently we added the Darby Rimmer Motor Neurone Disease Foundation. Stephen Darby, who played for Liverpool, Bolton and Bradford, has become a good friend, along with his wife Steph Houghton. Stephen has been so inspirational since he was diagnosed with MND. It was a pleasure to be able to make a donation to his foundation.

Amy has run marathons and half-marathons to raise

money, but she would tell you that organising the foundation's annual ball is even more demanding. That's where we raise most of our money. It's a huge event and we've had different themes over the years – New York, Las Vegas, Nightmare at Christmas, Willy Wonka's Chocolate Factory and so on – and we've had some great entertainment. We've had Gary Barlow, Olly Murs, Kaiser Chiefs. We've had Dynamo and other magicians, plus dodgems and waltzers at the end of the night. There are 500 or 600 people there, and it's like organising a huge wedding every year, sorting out the seating plan and the entertainment and getting people to support us with prizes, which so many generous people help us with.

Manchester City and Liverpool and all my team-mates at both clubs have been amazing with the support they've given the foundation. It would be a lot harder to do what I've done if I was at a club that didn't have the same resources or the same pull or the same commitment to helping people. Jürgen Klopp has been unbelievably generous in the support he has given the foundation. I have got so much respect for him for that – never mind for being a great football manager.

There are so many people who help us, but it's a lot of work, particularly for Amy, my agent Matthew and the people at Entertainment Today, who do a great job helping to organise it. Every year, it's bigger than the one before and every year there's probably a moment where we ask ourselves, 'Is this worth it?' And then the night comes along and there are so many people who have come to support it and raise money, and then we meet the people from the charities and we watch the short film about all the work that is being done and Amy and I look at each other and say, 'Yes, it's definitely worth it.'

A lot of people face difficulties from the very start of their lives. If you're lucky enough to be born with the opportunity to do something that others would love to be able to do, then I think you have a duty to do everything you can to try to make the most of that opportunity. If you can then take the opportunity to try to help other people who aren't so fortunate, then that's perfect.

Acknowledgements

This is one book that certainly wouldn't have been possible to produce without a lot of help -- especially from all those who provided the questions for me to answer. There were hundreds and hundreds, many of them not relating to Ribena, so thank you to all who posted questions, including those which didn't quite make the cut.

I would also like to thank my agent Matthew Buck for talking me into this project; David Luxton for coming up with the original idea; Oliver Kay for helping to piece it together; Matt McCann for his advice and input; Richard Milner (no relation) and his team at Quercus for publishing the book.

Thank you to all the team-mates, coaches and managers I have worked with over my years in football. A small number of them are mentioned in this book, but thank you also to those I haven't mentioned.

Above all thank you to my family: to Mum and Dad for all the support you have given me down the years; to my sister Claire, plus Gary and Tammy; and, last but definitely not least, to Amy, Holly and Zac. As a family we like to keep a low profile, but I don't think I will get many opportunities to thank them for everything they bring to my life. That moment I had on the pitch in Madrid with Amy and Claire, with the European Cup at our feet, and with Holly and Zac running around and picking confetti up off the pitch, will live with my family forever. That's what life has always come down to for me. Football and family. And winning, of course.

Picture Credits

Plate section images are © and courtesy of, in order of appearance:

1   John Walton/EMPICS Sport/PA Images
2   Matthew Impey/Shutterstock
3   Gareth Copley/PA Archive/PA Images
4   Mark Thompson/Getty Images
5, 6   Owen Humphreys/PA Archive/PA Images
7   Allstar Picture Library / Alamy Stock Photo
8   Sean Dempsey/PA Archive/PA Images
9   Stuart Franklin/Getty Images
10   Julian Finney/Getty Images
11   Ben Queenborough/Shutterstock
12   Michael Regan/Getty Images
13   Dave Thompson/PA Archive/PA Images
14   Clive Brunskill/Getty Images
15   Nick Potts/PA Wire/PA Images
16   Shaun Botterill/Getty Images
17   Marc Atkins/Getty Images
18   Nick Taylor/Liverpool FC/Liverpool FC via Getty Images
19   John Powell/Liverpool FC via Getty Images